Technology for the Language Classroom

Technology for the Language Classroom

Creating a Twenty-first-century Learning Experience

Leonardo A. Mercado
Academic Director, Euroidiomas

Applied Linguistics for the Language Classroom
Series Editor: Andy Curtis

First published 2017 by
PALGRAVE

Palgrave in the UK is an imprint of Macmillan Publishers Limited, registered in England, company number 785998, of 4 Crinan Street, London, N1 9XW.

Palgrave® and Macmillan® are registered trademarks in the United States, the United Kingdom, Europe and other countries.

ISBN: 978–1–137–49784–0 paperback

This book is printed on paper suitable for recycling and made from fully managed and sustained forest sources. Logging, pulping and manufacturing processes are expected to conform to the environmental regulations of the country of origin.

A catalogue record for this book is available from the British Library.

A catalog record for this book is available from the Library of Congress.

Printed in China

I dedicate this work to my loving family: my dear wife Nancy and my two beautiful children, Janella and Gabriel. I would also like to make a special mention of my loving mother, Eliana, and cherished father, Luis.

Contents

List of Figures and Tables

Figures

Tables

Series Editor's Introduction

The purpose of this Applied Linguistics for the Language Classroom (ALLC) series is to help bridge what still appears to be a significant gap between the field of applied linguistics and the day-to-day classroom realities of many language teachers and learners. For example, Selivan recently wrote that: "Much applied linguistics research remains unapplied, is often misapplied, or is downright inapplicable" (2016, p. 25). This gap appears to have existed for some time, and has yet to be bridged. For example, in 1954, Pulgram published *Applied Linguistics In Language Teaching*, which was followed a few years later by Robert Lado's classic work, *Linguistics Across Cultures: Applied Linguistics for Language Teachers* (1957). However, we are still seeing articles 60 years later helping language teachers to apply linguistic theory to language lessons (Magrath, 2016).

Therefore, one of the features of this ALLC series that makes it distinctive is our focus on helping to bridge the ongoing gap between applied linguistics and language classrooms. Our envisaged readership for these books is busy classroom language teachers, including those entering the profession and those who have been in it for some time already. We also gave a lot of thought to what teachers completing a first degree in Education, teachers doing MA TESOL courses, and language teachers completing other professional qualifications, would find most useful and helpful.

Bearing such readers in mind, one of the ambitious goals of this ALLC series is to present language teachers with clear, concise and up-to-date overviews and summaries of what they need to know in key areas: Assessment; Methods and

Methodologies; Technology; Research Methods; and Phonetics, Phonology and Pronunciation. Attempting to do what much larger and weightier volumes have attempted, but doing so in volumes that are slimmer and more accessible, has been a challenge, but we believe these books make an original and creative contribution to the literature for language teachers.

Another distinctive feature of this ALLC series has been our International Advisory Board, made up of Professor Kathleen Bailey and Professor David Nunan. These two outstanding figures in our field helped us to keep our target readers in mind and to stay focused on the classroom, while keeping the connections to applied linguistics, so we can advance the building of the bridges between applied linguistics and language classrooms.

For many of us, just keeping up with new and changing technologies can be a challenge in itself. Beyond that, finding the time to learn about these new technologies, so they can enhance the quality and the quantity of teaching and learning, presents another set of challenges. Leo Mercado understands such challenges well, based on many years of professional experience in a variety of different language education settings.

In *Technology for the Language Classroom*, Mercado starts with some fundamental questions: "What are today's learners like and how can we meet their needs? How can teachers get better prepared as facilitators of twenty-first century learning experiences? What should we look for in technology before using it?" (p. 2). In answering that last question, Mercado introduces the readers to a number of key considerations, including concepts such as 'massification', 'return on investment' and 'amenability', as well as 'scalability', 'manageability' and 'dependability' (Chapter 1).

In Chapter 2, Mercado considers more critical questions, including: "How do we integrate technology into the curriculum effectively?" (p. 22) and we are introduced to *millennials*, *digital natives*, and *net geners*, who are part of the new technological demographics seen more and more in today's language classrooms. Mercado has developed a number of new and innovative frameworks, such as his *Classroom and Autonomous Learning Integration* (CALI) concept, introduced in Chapter 1, and his *Quality Language Learning (QLL) Dynamics*, introduced in Chapter 2.

Interest in the autonomous or self-directed learning of students has continued to grow, as access to online technologies have grown, which is the focus of Chapter 3, where we learn about Mercado's LGOOS approach, based on Learning Goals, Objectives, Outcomes and Standards. In this chapter, we also explore survey results from a language school, which helps us understand more about why our learners study language online, as well as when and where they do their online studying.

In Chapter 4, Mercado introduces his idea of 'curricular vetting', which he describes as "a process by which contents are reviewed, evaluated, and primed for inclusion in a curriculum" (p. 70). Such vetting can be used to assess content for online and mobile learning. The tricky but important issue of 'authenticity' is also discussed in Chapter 4, plus sections on international benchmarks, and the research from applied linguistics in this area.

Focusing on specific language modalities and the development of second/foreign language skills, Chapter 5 looks at technologies to help develop listening and speaking skills, and Chapter 6 looks at reading and writing skills. Like all of the chapters in this book, these two contain many references to programs and applications that teachers can use with their students. There are also activities in every chapter to help teachers apply the theory to the practice, to see how things work in the 'real-life' of the classroom. And at the end of every chapter there are discussion questions, to help readers reflect, and suggested readings, with brief notes on each of the readings. There are also many diagrams, tables and other visual representations that help with the processing of the more technical content.

Chapter 7 looks at how technology can be employed to help students learn the grammar and the vocabulary of the target language, while Chapter 8 gives examples of technology used in the assessment, evaluation and proficiency testing of learners. The last Chapter (9) discusses how teachers can use technology in their own professional development.

Andy Curtis

Acknowledgements

I would like to thank those colleagues who made it possible for this book to have contributions from different countries and settings, including: Beth Bartlett, the academic director at the Centro Colombo Americano in Cali, Colombia; Nelson Jaramillo and Gina Vasquez, teachers from the Centro Colombo Americano in Cali, Colombia; Antonio Galimberti, teacher from Lima, Peru; Valeria Guerra and William Machado, teachers from Montevideo, Uruguay. I would also like to thank Ricardo Valle, the e-learning manager on my team at Euroidiomas in Lima, Peru who helped gather research data in support of content in the book.

Introduction

Looking back to the year 2003, I can recall the time when I was involved in research for my master's thesis, which focused on the application of technology to English language learning. At the time, it seemed like an excellent topic for study as computer-assisted language learning (CALL) was emerging as an important field, and little had yet been written on the subject. Searching for resources that could help me with the task, I found software that my institution had purchased at a tech exhibit during a TESOL Convention. It was collecting dust in a corner of the IT Department office, so I requested that I be allowed to use it on a trial basis. After some experimentation and much self-learning, I would use it with the students who participated in my thesis study. The work would later lead to the institution's first collection of online content for language practice, including a battery of exercises and activities that would familiarize students with a variety of international proficiency examinations. Once I became academic director two years later, I instituted the use of these resources for the official study programme and put together a team to create new content for all course and instructional levels. Eventually, educational technology for English language learning would become the focal point of my study and practice. Considering that I was in my mid-thirties at the time and that before then technology had not been such a fundamental pillar for my views on teaching and learning, I can be considered an example of a "late convert" of sorts to educational technology. Now, I am writing my second book on the subject; integrating technology into a variety of study programmes and projects for educational institutions, corporations and government organizations; and leading the development of online platforms, among other endeavours. The point I am trying to make is that it is never too early or too late to begin embracing technology for teaching and learning. Anyone can achieve success in becoming a successful ELT technology expert, and this book is set on helping its readers achieve that goal.

In writing this book, I have sought to find a balance between theory and practice. Certainly, theory and research are in and of themselves promising areas of study, but they must be applicable to classroom and virtual learning experiences if they are to be of any significant worth. Throughout the volume, you will find references to research in the field as well as studies in which I have been personally involved, extensive literature on the topics being presented, personal accounts of experiences that are relevant to the issues at hand as well as sample activities from real teachers who use technology successfully in different countries. One of the goals is to make certain that every idea and example presented in this book is based on something that has already been tried and tested for a successful outcome, particularly for teachers and learners but also for language programme administrators, curriculum writers, e-learning developers and other important stakeholders. In the end, it is my hope that this book serves not only as a source of practical ideas but also offers 'food for thought'. Another goal is for all relevant stakeholders who may find this book useful to come up with their own alternatives in order to explore the possibilities that technology offers, grounded as much as possible in a wide range of relevant research in applied linguistics as well as generally accepted pedagogical practice.

This book is divided into nine chapters. Chapter 1 sets the foundation for the entire volume by discussing the principles, concepts and factors that are most likely to contribute to a successful twenty-first-century learning experience, all of which are addressed repeatedly throughout the rest of the volume. Chapter 2 focuses on the use of technology in the classroom and presents a framework for teaching and learning that has technology as its main pillar. Chapter 3 defines autonomous learning and presents ways in which it can be promoted successfully, including references to successful blended learning programmes and other examples. Chapter 4 presents the many ways in which learning content, resources and tools for online and mobile-assisted language learning (MALL) can be vetted for more effective learning. Chapter 5 discusses speaking and listening skill development through technology, and Chapter 6 does the same for reading and writing. Chapter 7 addresses how technology can support the teaching and learning of language forms, specifically grammar, vocabulary and pronunciation. Chapter 8 focuses on assessment, evaluation and proficiency testing from a variety of perspectives, including classroom data collection, e-portfolios, international standards and accreditation, and even learning analytics. Finally, Chapter 9 discusses professional development for teachers through technology. In every chapter, there are practical activities to get teachers to put what they have read into practice in their own settings and contexts. Glossary terms are emphasized in bold where they are first used in the text, and are defined on page 203. Discussion questions have the purpose of engaging teachers in classroom or rap session discussions, one-to-one interactions with colleagues and mentors, and personal reflection. Again, the themes, principles and concepts presented in Chapter 1 are interwoven throughout the rest of the volume.

This book aims to help teachers, both new and experienced, discover how technology can positively transform their professional experiences and make successful learning through technology a common and welcome occurrence for their students. I set out to make it as practical and useful as possible, knowing that teachers need real-world ideas that can actually work. Yet, the book also has a strong grounding in research and literature pertinent to the field, because knowing *what* to do and *how* to do it is not enough unless these are accompanied by an understanding of *why* something is likely to work. In the end, it is my hope that you find the book very useful and that it serves to inspire a yearning to explore the seemingly endless potential for learning that technology can afford us.

CHAPTER 1

The Twenty-first-century Learning Experience

> Education is in an interesting transitional phase between its 'ICT-free' past and its 'ICT-aware' future.
>
> Laurillard, 2013, xx

In our twenty-first-century world, new information and communication technologies (ICTs) are emerging at an astonishing pace. Organizations are investing vast sums of money in research and development in order to find novel solutions to humankind's ever-changing needs and challenges. In the field of education, the fervour for achieving technological breakthroughs in such a short space of time is perhaps not as discernable, but significant progress has occurred nonetheless. Thus, few would argue against the notion that learning today is much different from what it was ten or even five years ago. As for present and future trends in education, a number of studies have shed light on technologies that seem to hold the most promise (Briggs, 2013), with enormous implications for the fields of second-language acquisition and English language teaching. In fact, these studies confirm that there is an almost immeasurable new expanse for learning that has yet to be explored. As such, gamification, **learning analytics**, flipped classrooms, cloud computing, virtual worlds, tablet-based apps and other technologies will soon be changing the mainstream English language training (ELT) landscape, leading to a new kind of language learning experience that meets the needs and demands of the twenty-first century. Consequently, our immediate thoughts are centred on the following questions, which are addressed throughout the chapter:

- What are today's learners like, and how can we meet their needs?
- How can teachers be better prepared as facilitators of twenty-first-century learning experiences?
- What should we look for in technology before using it?

The Oxford Dictionary (2015) defines **technology** as 'the application of scientific knowledge for practical purposes, especially in industry' or 'machinery and devices developed from scientific knowledge'. Throughout this book, technology is understood as digital or electronically based devices, resources or processes that facilitate the teacher and learners' ability to think, perform and succeed.

In this highly technological, so-called 'post-methods' era (Richards and Rogers, 2014; Thornbury, 2009), researchers, materials developers and classroom practitioners are exploring new perspectives on language learning, with prospects that seem more favourable than ever before. Technology now affords learners new ways to learn, practise and strategize while providing teachers with the means to make the instructional process more diverse, effective, efficient, engaging and contextually meaningful. What is so exciting for the field at this time is that there is undoubtedly an enormous opportunity to further explore the applicability of technology to the second-language acquisition process and English language teaching. Research can aid this effort by offering valuable insights into everyday instructional practices and student learning. The lessons learned can then be either applied directly or extrapolated by the intended end user.

In the search for ideas, solutions and innovations, technology can facilitate the English language learning process by making it more amenable and relevant to twenty-first-century learners, if it is applied wisely. Thus, key stakeholders in the educational process are called upon to make the right decisions as to which technologies should be used, as well as when and how. Curriculum and materials developers, including publishers and e-learning providers, must create content and learning opportunities that are engaging. In order to do so, the content should be in accordance with learners' needs, expectations and lifestyles, taking full advantage of technology as an important recourse. Applied linguists have the all-important role of working closely with these other constituent groups in order to unveil and propose new practices that may lead to more effective and efficient paths to learning, with technology in a supporting role. They must also make certain that any perceived gains are grounded in solid, objective data. Thus, to ensure that technology serves its purpose well and offers the greatest possible gains, all of the stakeholders depicted in Figure 1.1 should work closely together in order to have the

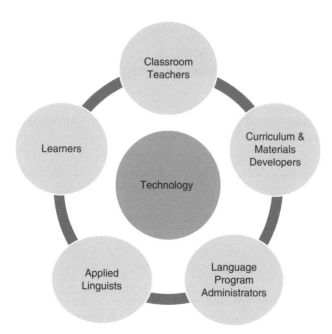

Figure 1.1 Collaborative cycle for major stakeholders in a twenty-first-century technological era.

greatest impact on the learning process. They should share information, experiences and ideas whenever possible. Let us not forget the learners, who also play an important role by offering input and feedback on what they think works and what they most like. Substantive new gains in the field of English language learning will not be possible without such collaboration.

Opportunities for engaging in research and innovative practices in English language learning through technology are countless. Perhaps it would be wise for these efforts to be concentrated on those areas that have the greatest potential for advancing the field, with an emphasis on those aspects of the teaching and learning process that may be of greatest interest to the everyday practitioner. Table 1.1 provides a list of areas on which research and exploratory practice could focus over the coming years in the hope of revealing new paths to learner achievement and proficiency development.

Table 1.1 Areas for Research and Exploratory Practice with the Greatest Potential

Opportunities for Research and Practice in Technology and ELT	
Area	**Potential**
Motivation	Align the learning experience with the learner's background, preferences, goals and self-concept to make it more meaningful and relevant.
Skills	Find new ways to develop the learners' language, higher-order and technological skills, thus helping them attain a more complete competency profile.
Proficiency Standards and Benchmarks	Establish a strong correspondence between learner achievement and international proficiency benchmarks, including technology standards, in order to make their skill and knowledge sets more robust, comparable across different settings and contexts, and applicable to the world outside the classroom.

Content-Based Instruction (CBI) / Content and Language Integrated Learning (CLIL)	Facilitate the acquisition of language skills through content that is contextualized in the form of subject matter that is not ESL/EFL oriented, responding to more recent trends that concentrate on large amounts of differentiated input, life skills for professional and academic contexts, and vocabulary building.
Autonomous, 'Situational' and 'Instinctive' Learning	Create new spaces and opportunities for learning through which the learner can significantly expand the classroom learning experience.
Learner Achievement	Develop novel means to assess, monitor, analyse and report on learner achievement in order to improve instruction and learning.

Motivation and Development

The process of learning a second or foreign language is long, complex and highly dependent on a range of variables, of which learner motivation is perhaps the most crucial. As Brown (2007) points out, 'countless studies and experiments in human learning have shown that motivation is a key to learning in general' (p. 168). Krashen (1982) also highlights learner motivation as one of the attitudinal factors that has the greatest effect on language-acquisition success. To promote the highest degree of learner motivation, however, teachers must fully understand the needs and expectations of their students and what is most likely to keep them engaged throughout the entire learning process. This means it is an

ACTIVITY

Create an instrument that will allow you to collect information on your students' satisfaction with a technological device, resource or activity. Then develop an action plan to follow up.

absolute must for English language teachers to familiarize themselves with the likes and preferences of the twenty-first-century learners they will find in their classrooms. Recognizing that these learners expect technology to be an integral part of their language learning experiences is essential for success.

Today, many teachers may find that a majority of learners in their class are composed of members of the millennial generation and 'digital natives' (Prensky, 2001), groups which have been found to have a great reliance on technology for activities in their everyday lives. For Hershatter and Epstein (2010), **millennials** have adopted technology as a 'sixth sense' that serves as the principal means through which they interact with the world. Going further, Wilson and Gerber (2008) refer to research findings that highlight the enormous preference millennials have for technological applications, including video games, and how this has major implications for language teaching pedagogy in terms of goal setting, task completion, intrinsic motivation, feedback and rewards. As regards these **digital natives**, Prensky (2011) reminds us that the key to the future of education is not so much whether we use technology, but how we use it and to what extent that reflects our students' fast-paced, highly connected view of the world.

Bennett (2012), however, warns us not to take anything for granted, referring to many studies that have been conducted since Prensky's first article. Most of these indicate that the term *digital natives* may not be as generalizable to a certain age group as was initially claimed. In fact, it may apply in its truest sense to only a small minority of that population due to the existence of 'digital divides', or notable disparities in terms of which technologies are accessible or how technology is used. Therefore, it is essential for teachers to adapt technology and apply it so that it matches the learners' backgrounds and characteristics as closely as possible, depending on the group, setting or **context.** To achieve success, however, it may not be enough to know who our learners are; we must also know what motivates them.

In today's globalized world, English undoubtedly continues to grow in importance as the main means of international communication, with an estimated 2 to 3 billion people using or learning the language around the world (Crystal, 2008; Graddol, 2006). In L2 (second-language) motivation research and literature, this is often attributed to the notion that language learners wish to connect with the world as *global citizens*, a term that has arisen from the gradual diminishing of barriers previously imposed by geographic location and a lack of technology. Gardner and Lambert's (1972) concept of *integrativeness* seems to support this view, stating that the motivation of language learners is strongly grounded in their desire to get closer psychologically to another language community or cultural group. However, other motivation researchers have a different perspective (Ushioda and Dörnyei, 2009; Ryan, 2006), often citing a person's desire to develop a self-concept or sense of identity rather than identification with an external reference group (Ushioda and Dörnyei). Markus and Nurius (1986), for example, have proposed the existence of *possible selves*, or the language learners' present conceptualizations of what they might become, what they would like to become and what they are afraid of becoming.

Another mainstream view of L2 motivation is that communicating in English has become a necessity for accessing opportunities in life and raising living standards, especially in countries where it is taught as a foreign language. Graddol (2006) affirms this is due to economic motives that arise from the presence of transnational corporations throughout the globe, as well as the drive of many countries to become more competitive on the world stage. He goes further to say that English 'is widely regarded as a gateway to wealth for national economies, organizations, and individuals. If that is correct, the distribution of poverty in the future will be closely linked to the distributions of English' (p. 38). Thus, English can be seen as a commodity, affording a high status to those individuals within a society who can use it satisfactorily and conferring the power to advance their self-interests (Tan and Rubdy, 2008).

In the professional world, English is considered by many to be a universal life skill. The International Research Foundation for English Language Education (TIRF), for example, recently sponsored a large-scale, global study to identify the knowledge and skills required for the twenty-first-century workplace. The study concluded that language learning experiences are shifting towards the mastery of 'competencies which will enable [language learners] to communicate and collaborate with others, organize and analyze information, make informed decisions, and take decisive action in professional contexts' (Fitzpatrick and O'Dowd, 2012, p. 20).

Despite the wide variety of perspectives in academia, classroom practitioners may not need an in-depth knowledge of the research and literature to successfully approach L2 motivation within a twenty-first-century, highly technological context. Perhaps it is sufficient for teachers to understand that their students are learning the target language in an era of globalization. This means that it is very likely that at some point they will encounter English speakers from different parts of the world without leaving their own countries, cities or even their offices and homes, not to mention the endless amount of cultural input from around the globe that is now accessible in English via cable television and the Internet. Moreover, the instrumental purpose of learning the language is fast becoming an unavoidable reality that goes beyond freedom of choice of the language learner. For example, many universities in EFL settings now require English for graduation, regardless of the personal preferences for language learning their students may have. Similarly, many companies have established degrees of competency in English as prerequisites for higher-end, better-paying jobs (Neely, 2012).

In terms of self-identity, teachers have long been aware of the need to recognize students as individuals, each with their own personal needs, goals, challenges and dreams. Technology allows the language learners to personalize their education in the language. It takes it above and beyond the standardized, one-size-fits-all approach that still characterizes many language classrooms today. With technology as a foundation, the following could be taken into consideration when it comes to maximizing learner motivation, taking as a reference the theoretical constructs we have discussed so far (Table 1.2):

Table 1.2 L2 Motivation Research Constructs, with Implications in Terms of Pedagogy and Technology

L2 Motivation Construct	Examples of Supporting Technology
Integrativeness	Social media, MOOCs, blogs, wikis, mobile apps and content management platforms can all provide learners with vast amounts of input in the L2 that can reinforce their identification with or desire to learn more about a target language user group or culture. They can also offer channels of communication with their classmates as well as learners from other groups, cities and countries.
Self-Identity	Virtual worlds, such as *Second Life*®, can offer language learners the possibility of assuming alternative, desirable selves. Learning analytics technology allows learners to monitor their progress and set learning goals that are in line with their current and future needs. Modern learning management systems (LMSs) and educational apps can allow learners to personalize their daily lessons and build up readily accessible e-portfolios of their achievements as they strive to attain a future state of being.
Instrumental	Content platforms can provide learning content, assessments and resources to support English for academic or professional purposes. Virtual environments and laboratories can serve as venues for practising essential life skills. Cloud technology allows students to upload their work, content, etc., at any time during their very busy lives.

Thus far, we have answered the first question posed at the beginning of the chapter. As a result, it is clear that knowing our learners and promoting their motivation are both essential to the success of any language learning experience. Yet, we must also keep in mind that teacher motivation and self-confidence are equally important. When teachers are motivated, they make a greater effort to understand their learners' wants, needs and expectations, as well as create a learning environment that maximizes learner engagement and commitment. They are also more likely to be open to change and innovative practice, including the use of technology. The opposite also holds true as well. Teachers who tend to show negative attitudes or dispositions will often be less likely to engage in the kind of self-reflection and self-determination that may be critical for overcoming their fear of change, as some studies seem to indicate (Bitner and Bitner, 2002; Villegas, 2007).

For many teachers, coming to terms with the use of technology in their classrooms can still represent a major concern and cause of anxiety. Blended and fully virtual learning solutions, for example, are now quite common and can be seen by teachers as a threat to their careers (Blake, 2008). In addition, the seemingly endless emergence of new technologies in the form of devices, operating systems, apps, content management platforms and web-based resources can be difficult to keep up with and sometimes overwhelming. Perhaps for such teachers, the often-quoted 'Technology won't replace teachers, but teachers who use technology will probably replace teachers who don't' is representative of their fears that their unfamiliarity with technological tools and resources will eventually be reflected in an unfavourable comparison with their more tech-savvy colleagues. Therefore, even in the second decade of the twenty-first century, it is highly probable that fully integrating technology into the English language learning experience is still an enormous challenge for many teachers.

According to various studies, there is a close relationship between teachers' beliefs, attitudes and dispositions towards technology and their potential for success in applying it to the classroom. Teachers who exhibit positive dispositions towards change and innovation will generally be the most open to the idea of creating a highly technological learning experience for their students. In a study with 12 award-winning, highly technology-proficient teachers, the findings showed that there can be a high degree of alignment between teachers' beliefs and attitudes about using technology with their actual practices. This has clear implications for learning that can be highly positive when teachers embrace technology as a powerful tool (Ertmer et al., 2012). From the perspective of motivation theory, Sokolowski and Heckhausen (2010) point out that teachers will embrace technology if: (i) the goals they have set for themselves are plausible and hold a positive emotional value that is associated with some form of personal gain; (ii) the negative consequences associated with not making the effort are significant; and (iii) the expectations placed on them by their authorities are reasonable.

Contrary to what some may believe, teachers need not become experts in the use of technology as soon as they begin their careers or new jobs. As with all other aspects of teaching, it takes time to develop a level of expertise that can provide confidence about its use. Along with a growing knowledge of technological devices, tools and resources, a repertoire of *strategies for learning enhancement through technology*, or **SLET** (Mercado, 2012a), can be developed as experience is gained. Such strategies involve the use of technology to improve classroom management, student interactions, levels of engagement, the

ACTIVITY

For a week, track the number of times you use technology in your lessons, and reflect on why you used it. Did you have a strong reason for each use? How did it impact each lesson?

presentation of new language, skill practice, personalization, knowledge transfer and more. To maximize their chances of success, teachers should start off slowly by limiting the scope of the technology and strategies they wish to employ. Once they have met their own expectations for success, they can gradually expand the number of alternatives. Here is a possible path to developing expertise in the use of SLET:

- Stage 1: The teacher uses technology to facilitate classroom management and delivery of content (e.g. YouTube, PowerPoint, websites, timing with digital stopwatches, interactive whiteboards (IWBs), etc.)
- Stage 2: The teacher uses technology to promote autonomous learning (e.g. Google Group online forums and communities, LMSs, content management platforms, websites, mobile apps and *autonomous learning projects*, or ALPs (Mercado, 2015b).
- Stage 3: The teacher and learners collaborate in making the learning experience more technological in nature by jointly creating or contributing to wiki's, blogs, newsletters, community service projects, mutual sharing forums and so on.

The stages are not necessarily sequential. Teachers may be able to engage in activities that are associated with more than one stage, especially as they accrue experience and become more confident. However, teachers who are new to this kind of technology, or who have decided to gradually build up their repertoire of SLET from what may currently be an elementary knowledge and skill set, can begin with the first stage. This could mean, for example, using a YouTube video of their own, a digital stopwatch to improve lesson pacing and student participation, or Microsoft PowerPoint to present a grammar or vocabulary lesson rather than using the board. These are relatively simple tasks that require little training or effort. At Stage 2, however, teachers do need additional preparation, practice, familiarity and/or training to use, for example, LMSs, Skype and Google Group (e.g. recording feature, aligning classroom and autonomous tasks – covered in Chapter 4). For Stage 3, teachers need to be working in a highly collaborative classroom environment, the creation of which is a demanding process in and of itself, along with using the respective specifications, procedures and protocols for content development, tools, resources and so forth.

When working on their lesson plans, teachers should map out the opportunities for technology to play a supporting role for learning enhancement or classroom management.

Context

Context could be understood as a current, desired or anticipated situation or state that serves as a frame of reference for language use in any of its forms (e.g. words, phrases, sentences, etc.). From a linguistic and pedagogically oriented perspective, contextualization is perhaps the factor that has the most impact on the success of any language learning experience. Many would probably say that it is the key to language learning. Nunan (1999a) refers to it as extra linguistic knowledge and knowledge of the world, without which language cannot even be understood, much less serve a functional purpose. Nation (2008b) considers guessing the meaning of new words from context as one of the most important of all vocabulary learning strategies. The stakeholders, the educational setting, the type of instruction and assessment in the classroom, and other factors play a crucial role in contextualizing the language for test design, implementation and subsequent washback (Cheng and Curtis, 2004). From the broader view of second-language acquisition research, it is believed that making certain a full range of contexts are provided for L2 output or target language use will give learners a reason to attend to the language and do their best to offer what Ellis (2005) calls a 'full performance' (p. 41) that reflects their ability to handle diverse situations. Krashen (1982) has referred to context as an essential means of scaffolding L2 input, thus making it more comprehensible.

In the twenty-first century, technology is a key channel through which the context of language can be communicated and deciphered. Technology has the potential to bring the target language to life in ways not possible before as students engage in their learning experiences, whether in a classroom, at home, on the bus, in a park or anywhere else an opportune learning moment may arise. In the past, most of the learning had to take place in the classroom, with highly graded, scaffolded input that often came as audio or video with the printed course book material. Now, the language can be contextualized on something as small and portable as a smartphone. Some examples include grammar exercises in an LMS for the kind of practice that focuses on form and seeks to prepare students for an international proficiency examination; input for **situated learning** (Beatty, 2013) on the street that comes through a useful app for daily reference; or, when available, in the form of apps like *Skype*, *Google Hangouts* or *Jitsi*, all of which make video chatting and conferencing with friends possible through their powerful voice over Internet protocol (VoIP) capabilities.

On the Internet, there are abundant resources as well. The British National Corpus or Brigham Young University's Corpus of Contemporary American English (COCA) or any other large collection of contextualized language provides language learners with hundreds of millions of examples of how language is used in a range of authentic, out-of-class settings. Similarly, DiVii is a powerful Internet-based application for use on either a personal computer or a mobile device that serves as a video dictionary, allowing students to find new words that are highlighted and embedded in thousands of authentic videos. Back in the classroom, the target language can now be contextualized faster than ever before through the use of audio and video files, Internet websites, mobile device apps, PowerPoint and Prezi presentations, IWBs, and so on.

The context of where the learning is to take place is also a fundamental factor to consider when trying to ascertain the applicability of technology. Nowadays, English language learning can take place at a school, university, binational centre, language academy or non-governmental organization (NGO). The degree of investment in technology, whether it is in the form of a Wi-Fi or cable Internet connection, bandwidth capability, IWBs, mobile devices, servers, multimedia labs and so on, will determine the degree to which the institution is willing and able to commit to a twenty-first-century learning experience for its students. However, at times, financial constraints do not allow for a wide-scale, varied implementation. Under such conditions, institutions should consider low-cost options that offer the greatest benefit in favour of an efficacious teaching and learning process. Here are some essential principles to keep in mind as we answer the question 'What should we look for in technology before using it?':

- *Massification*: It has to be able to reach and benefit the greatest number of students.
- *Return on investment (ROI)*: The benefits in terms of additional learning must offset the investment in time, effort and money by a significant margin.
- *Amenability*: Students should be able to relate to technology as meaningful and relevant to what they see and do in their daily lives.
- *Scalability*: Without requiring an additional investment, it can be applied upward, as the number of students grows, for a greater degree of individualization and personalized use, or downward, to be shared among a group.
- *Manageability*: It should be user-friendly for learners, teachers and even language programme administrators, who must decide on how to implement it for the best results.
- *Dependability*: It should be trustworthy so that it always (or almost always) works and is available when needed.
- *Appeal*: It should have innate characteristics that make it engaging for students to use.

An educational institution with ample financial resources would most likely make a substantial investment in order to ensure the availability of technology. IWBs in the classroom, Internet connectivity with a high bandwidth, tablets or laptops for students, a range of software and applications, and an organizational culture that promotes creativity with technology on the part of both students and teachers would be some of the benefits. These institutions have curricula in which the use of technology is integrated throughout the study programme and is considered essential for student success. They will have a learning environment that not only focuses on learner achievement in the classroom but also one that promotes a high degree of autonomous student learning. In such cases, teachers will make it a habit to engage in exploratory teaching through technology and share ideas and resources with their colleagues. They will be highly versed in SLET and trained constantly. Rather than resorting mainly to face-to-face instruction, blended learning and flipped classrooms may be more of the norm in such institutions.

In the case of institutions with limited funds, the approach to using technology may be highly conservative. For example, there may be a small number of personal computers, laptops or tablets that must be shared by the students, either in the classroom or in a multimedia lab, if there is one; limited Internet capability/access; and an organizational culture that provides its students with occasional exposure to technology rather than making its use a permanent characteristic of the learning experience. The challenge for teachers and language programme administrators in such situations is finding a way to take full advantage of opportunities as they arise, especially since proficiency in the use of technology has become such a necessity. Language programme administrators and other key authorities who are entrusted with acquiring technology and making it available should ensure at least periodic access. They should also guide teachers on how to use technology effectively and efficiently in order to achieve clearly identified goals and objectives. Here are some ideas for such institutions:

ACTIVITY

Students can be taken on field trips to places in which technology abounds. They could go to a museum with interactive information panels, the library for research, or visit a highly technological 'brother' or 'sister' school so that the students from both institutions can engage research or science fairs, 'swap meets' or other interactive activities. Regardless of how much your technology your institution employs, consider one of these options as a novel way to make your classes more interesting.

- *Sharing*: Students should share the personal computers, laptops, tablets or smartphones that may be available. It may not be possible or necessary for all students to have their own devices. The lesson plan should account for this and ensure that all students have an equal opportunity to use whatever devices are available. Students should be informed in advance of the nature and purpose of the activity that will require such sharing.
- *Alternate means*: If the educational institution cannot afford to invest in a permanent multimedia lab, it may be possible to rent certain equipment for specific days each month.
- *Adaptation*: Classrooms with low bandwidth for an Internet connection will have difficulties buffering videos and other dynamic content from the web. In those contexts, teachers could use websites and previously downloaded content, including pictures and videos, to avoid unnecessary delays during the lesson.
- *Partnerships and grants*: Institutions can seek partnerships with other educational organizations and government agencies that have greater technological resources, so that students can make use of them at different times during the year. Grants could also be sought in order to finance the acquisition of new equipment and resources, train teachers on the use of technology and fund other projects.

Selecting the Right Technology

As a whole, technology has been used in the field of education and in English language teaching since the 1980s, with an exploding array of new alternatives just over the past few years. Unfortunately, it has not always been purchased or used wisely, at times resulting in million-dollar losses without a significant return in the form of benefits for the language learner. As an example, one Latin American government acquired more than 100,000 IWBs for distribution among the country's public schools. This was a good initiative. Unfortunately, many teachers were never trained on their use, and the devices were even distributed to places with no electricity (Color ABC, 2009).

What is important to keep in mind is that technology does not guarantee learning outcomes on its own. It will only become a powerful enabler and enhancer of the learning experience if the key stakeholders in the educational process use it with enough knowledge, expertise and determination. There must also be a conscientious effort on the part of institutional authorities to expand the learning envelope beyond the traditional paradigm of classroom teaching and learning. Using technology, it is possible to empower English language learners so that they can continue learning, practising and consolidating their language skills outside of a formal educational setting whenever they choose to do so. By promoting learner self-determination, learners will be able to choose what, when and how they want to learn. Moreover, when educational authorities espouse the concept of **classroom and autonomous learning integration (CALI)** (Mercado, 2015b), which is the systematic and purposeful integration of classroom learning and autonomous learning processes, a potentially boundless expanse of new opportunities for students to learn and practise the language is created.

Successful experiences with technology can shed light on the kinds of decisions that key stakeholders can make in order to bring about the greatest possible positive impact. Every context is unique, but often the ultimate aim for using a particular technology is generally the same regardless of context or setting. As an example, such an experience took place when I was director at a language centre in Latin America. In 2005, we had to decide on a new technology to implement in the study programme as part of our efforts to renovate the learning experience for our students. The challenge was to choose a technology that could be acquired at the lowest possible cost and yet be widely implemented to benefit the greatest number of students. The alternatives offered by the competing publishers were (i) an online e-workbook; (ii) digital IWBs with supporting software; and (iii) a CD-ROM to go with one of the contending course books. After reviewing the research, consulting renowned experts in the field and doing a financial analysis, we chose the e-workbook option because of its scalability, low cost and usefulness in promoting autonomous learning, something which was consistent with the institution's new educational philosophy. Because it was Internet based, massification was more than feasible. The IWB option was postponed for reconsideration at a later date because of the high acquisition and maintenance costs at the time and the concern that it would inadvertently lead to greater teacher-talk-time in detriment to student-talk-time. The CD-ROM option was considered too traditional and passé. Looking back, the fact that as many as 70 per cent of the tens of thousands of students (*note*: reference to number is to highlight the impact of the decision and of using appropriate technology) enrolled there regularly got to use the *e-workbook* and other web-based resources indicates it was the right decision.

Conclusion

In this chapter, I have set out to make the point that technology must be an integral part of twenty-first-century language learning experience because learners, as digital natives and millennials, expect it to be so. Yet technology is but a means to an end and should be chosen and used carefully if it is to truly help our learners reach their fullest potential in learning a second language. In the end, choosing the right technology depends on what its ROI of sorts will be: how do the learning and other benefits for our students offset the investment in time, money and effort made by all of the key stakeholders in the process?

This first chapter establishes the underlying philosophy and aims for the entire book. As you think of how the ideas in this book can be applied in your classroom, you may see that, in talking about technology, we are also touching on issues such as learner motivation, CALI and the contextualization of language, among others. Therefore, it will become evident throughout the rest of the volume that the proposed strategies and innovations for enhancing English language learning through technology are all grounded – to one extent or another – in the principles, concepts and beliefs presented in this first chapter.

Discussion Questions

1. Of the different areas in technology that offer encouraging prospects for second-language acquisition and English language teaching research, which one would you like to explore on your own? How?
2. In your opinion, what are three things to keep in mind when thinking about maximizing English language learner motivation through the use of technology? How can you include them in your lesson planning?
3. How would you rate your current level of expertise in applying SLET? What do you feel is the next step you need to take in your professional development in this area?
4. Imagine you have limited technological resources in your English language class. What are some strategies you would use in order to maximize learner participation and achievement?
5. Can you give an example of how the context provided in a course book activity could be enhanced through technology?

6. How would you offer your students the opportunity to communicate with L2 learners in another city or country? How would that be integrated into your lesson or curriculum?

Suggested Readings

Beetham, H. and R. Sharpe (2013) *Rethinking Pedagogy for a Digital Age* (New York and Oxon: Routledge).
Orients teachers towards changing their philosophies on teaching and learning to account for technology.

Dörnyei, Z. and E. Ushioda (2009) *Motivation, Language Identity, and the L2 Self* (Bristol: Multilingual Matters).
Helps teachers better understand learner motivation so it can be enhanced through technology.

Prensky, M. (2010) *Teaching Digital Natives: Partnering for Real Learning* (Washington, DC: Sage).
Guides teachers on how to work effectively with today's 'digital natives'.

2 # The Classroom as a Technology Centre

> *How do we educate the 'new child,' raised in a world of instant information, where interactive technologies have led them to believe they can act on the world with the press of a button?*
> Strommen and Lincoln, 1992, p.467

The quote above was from more than 20 years ago, at a time when technologies that seem so commonplace today were just emerging. In their discussion, Strommen and Lincoln stressed the need to bridge the divide between the typical teaching and learning experience of the time and what was expected to become the classroom of the future. Such an effort would call for 'a guiding philosophy that suggests principled changes in the curriculum, and effective uses of technology as part of these changes' (p. 467). It would be an effective means of accounting for the rapid transformation taking place in society at the time, and parting with an educational system that was apparently locked in the past. In relation, some questions come to mind:

- Where are we today?
- How do we integrate technology into the curriculum effectively?
- Is it enough simply to introduce technology? What about our ways of thinking?

Even in this day and age, despite the fact that we find ourselves immersed in a world full of technology, the classroom continues to be the principal venue for most formal language learning experiences. Extensive research supports the idea that social interaction is vital to second language acquisition (Ellis, 1999; Gass, Mackey, and Pica, 1998; Lantolf, Thorne, and Poehner, 2014), so few would argue that technology could ever make the classroom unnecessary, much less eliminate the need for one of its main protagonists: the teacher. In the classroom, simulations of 'real-life' situations, socialization among learners and efforts to communicate successfully in the L2 all centre on the teacher's direction, something that is seemingly more difficult to achieve when learners work autonomously in a virtual environment. Despite the Internet, cable television and other communication media, the classroom is likely still the place from which the greatest amount and variety of a language learner's comprehensible input in the language is obtained, whether it comes from course book content, graded audio and video, the teacher or classmates. Teachers can provide 'real-world', contextualized examples of how language is used outside of an instructional setting, or greatly facilitate such searches. When new grammar or pronunciation features are not well understood, the teacher is called upon to clarify, explain or model, and no computer-generated feedback yet in existence can fulfil that role to the same degree of efficacy. Finally, the classroom provides learners with a convenient space in which they can meet regularly outside of their very busy lives and fully concentrate on their learning. Despite all of these virtues, however, classroom learning may be subject to inefficiencies and fall short of stakeholder expectations. Fortunately, technology can play an important role in overcoming such challenges by enabling and enhancing those factors that are most likely to contribute to language learning success.

Technology has enormous potential as a powerful tool and resource, but introducing it into the classroom without a proper vetting process is ill advised, especially in this day and age. In an era of standards and high stakes assessments, teachers are perhaps more accountable for their students' learning than ever before. International proficiency **benchmarks**, such as the

Common European Framework of Reference for Languages (CEFR), TESOL K–12, World Class Instructional Design and Assessment (WIDA), and the American Council on the Teaching of Foreign Languages (ACTFL) Proficiency Guidelines, describe the language competencies and skills learners should possess at different stages of their language development. Expectations for learning are often based on the number of class contact hours to which students have been exposed in a formal study programme and the proficiency examinations they are able to pass as a result (Desveaux, 2015; Mercado, 2012b; O'Maggio-Hadley, 2001). Consequently, efficiency and effectiveness of the learning process become an absolute priority. From a teacher's perspective, it means that every minute of every lesson must be exploited to its fullest in order to advance language learning, practice and consolidation. Yet the challenges for teachers are many, and they tend to be associated with those aspects of the learning process in which the teachers' actions, or lack thereof, have the greatest impact. This explains why the correct selection and use of technology is so vital.

A Twenty-first-century Framework

Learners are often engaged in a constant evaluation of their teachers, lessons, materials, classroom environment, technologies and resources. Learners want to feel like their time is being spent profitably and that the learning endeavour is worthwhile. Consequently, institutions should make certain that once learners embark on a learning experience, they should sense that their goals are being met and that they are making substantial progress, which becomes more noticeable as the investment in time increases. Research studies have shown, however, that if learners cannot perceive a relation between their efforts and acceptable outcomes, amotivation can set in, making them lose the desire to continue with the learning endeavour simply because they do not expect to achieve success or they no longer see the value in the language learning process overall (Vandergrift, 2005). On the other hand, numerous studies highlight the positive attitudes that can result from perceived end-of-training proficiencies in the language (i.e. speaking, reading, etc.) and other forms of L2 achievement (Noels, Pelletier and Vallerand, 2000). Motivation theorists remind us that 'individuals' choice, persistence and performance can be explained by their beliefs about how well they will do on an activity and the extent to which they value the activity' (Wigfield and Eccles, 2000, p. 68).

Ultimately, language-learning success will provide learners with the motivation to continue with their studies. Even so, maintaining a high level of motivation is no easy task. As Karaoglu (2015) points out, 'Motivation fluctuates, and it is challenging to keep language learners' motivation at a high level all the time' (p. 4). Ideally, learners and teachers should be immersed in a highly positive emotional state, much like the one Csikszentmihalyi (2014) calls 'flow', in which willing involvement, energized activity and ultimate enjoyment serve as the catalysts for optimal learning and performance. Dörnyei (1994) refers to the effect course materials, teaching methods and learning tasks may have on learners. He also cites teacher-specific variables, such as instructors' personality, teaching style and the relationship they have with their students. Finally, the level and nature of the interactions among groups of students can play an important role as well.

In the search for the twenty-first-century classroom, it would seem that there are additional macro-level variables that can greatly influence learner engagement and motivation. The first is *time*, which characterizes the length of exposures to L2 input, L2 output turns, activities, tasks and any other event that has the purpose of fostering language learning and prac-tice. When too much or too little time is allotted, chances are there will be a negative effect on learner performance and dis-positions. The second is what I would call *event codification*, which essentially means that learners will process and codify all stimuli and situations during the lesson to determine their relevance in terms of their own needs, wants and aims. The greater the proportion of relevant events and positive critical incidents to total class time, the greater the degree of 'buy in' and willingness on the part of the learner to collaborate with the learning experience. Needless to say, there is a greater chance that learners will become disengaged when lessons are not deemed of value to their own personal interests. Finally, *delivery* is another all-important variable that is mainly up to the teacher, although learners share some of the responsibility for it in collaborative classroom environments. As with any good presentation, delivery is essential for maintaining the interest of an audience, except that in this case the audience consists of a classroom full of learners. What I am affirming is that learners expect their teacher to be entertaining, organized, confident and convincing. The smoother the flow of activities and tasks, the clearer the explanations and instructions; and the more pleasant the classroom environment, the more the learners will commit to their 'part of the deal'. This requires an ample repertoire of effective instructional strategies, an amenable and visibly effective teaching style and innate characteristics on the part of the teacher, such as charisma, organization and resourcefulness. Learners must also present, perform and explain for the class, and their classmates will expect similar traits and virtues from them as well.

These are all factors twenty-first-century learners are likely to consider when comparing their daily classroom and multimedia language lab experiences to their own expectations. Hopefully, the result of each assessment is that they will be looking forward to the following day's lesson rather than abhor the prospect. Before creating effective, technologically empowered classrooms, however, institutions and teachers must first embrace a philosophy on teaching and learning that recognizes the special role technology plays in motivating today's twenty-first-century language learners and facilitate every means for them to succeed. This especially holds true when we are reminded of Strommen and Lincoln's (1992) call for a guiding philosophy more than twenty years ago. With all of the *millennials*, *digital natives* and *net geners* who have come to represent the majority of the students in our classrooms, it would probably make a great deal of sense to believe in and do our very best to make the most of the powers technology has to offer. The classroom, along with the multimedia language lab as its primary extension, becomes a place in which technology can thrive as an enabler of student learning. With a philosophy that advocates a continuous learning experience unbound by physical constraints, the classroom and autonomous learning integration (CALI) concept (Mercado, 2015b), introduced in the previous chapter, becomes a practical reality.

As a means of facilitating the integration of technology in the classroom while addressing all of these issues, I would like to propose what I call *Quality Language Learning (QLL) Dynamics* as a practical, simple-to-understand pedagogical framework for learning that has technology as its main pillar. In fact, I first introduced it in a more elementary, initial form several years ago at a very large language centre in Latin America, where I was the academic director. The central idea is that with a proficient use of technology in the classroom, classes should be more dynamic, flow more smoothly and be less predictable. Successful time management, delivery and event codification can all be enabled. There can be much technology or very little, but its presence must be felt regardless. This, in turn, will lead to higher levels of learner motivation and engagement as well as an increased likelihood that lessons will be deemed satisfactory at the end of the day. Technology can empower students to become co-contributors to the learning experience, allowing them to create content and provide learning prompts of their own. When it is well chosen, technology contributes to the development of all of the major language skill and knowledge areas. Finally, it can establish bridges that learners can use to continue learning on their

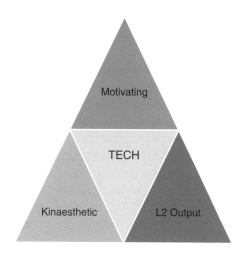

Figure 2.1 'Dynamics Triangle' for successful classroom learning within a QLL Dynamics framework.

own, opening up the opportunity to self-determined learning paths and an increased awareness of personal achievement. In such a classroom, teachers and learners know their roles well, collaborating to achieve mutually acceptable lesson outcomes.

As depicted in Figure 2.1, QLL Dynamics consists of several essential driving forces that serve to create the kind of fulfiling learning experience to which positive psychologists, such as Csikszentmihalyi, or educational thinkers, such as Dörnyei and Ushioda, so often refer. They are as follows:

- *Kinaesthetic dynamics*: systematic, ongoing actions in class that promote changes in the students' physical displacement in order to keep them from remaining sedentary and succumbing to boredom. Teachers can alternate seating arrangements and partners, or ask students to go to the board, perform in front of the class or circulate around the classroom for a communicative activity. These opportunities are constant and either planned carefully in advance or created on the spot during a lesson, whenever the teacher decides.

- *L2 output dynamics*: The determination on the part of the teacher to use – as much as possible – instructional strategies that promote 'high quality' or extensive learner practice in speaking and writing, such as think-pair-share, *classroom interaction techniques* (CITs) (Schwartz, 2001), freewriting, and the 4-3-2 technique (Arevart and Nation, 1991), among so many others. Another key aspect of *L2 Output Dynamics* is the maximization of the number of student-to-student (S–S) or teacher-to-student (T–S) interactions at any moment during a lesson, having the largest number of students participate in the shortest amount of time. For example, a teacher may have 70 to 100 per cent of the class participate by speaking with sustained, individual turns within a 90-second to 3-minute period. Overall, the teacher goes above and beyond to create opportunities for productive language practice.
- *Motivating dynamics*: Choosing the right topics and themes for students, providing interesting and helpful L2 content/input, using engaging activities and tasks, ensuring a pleasant classroom environment, maintaining positive attitudes and 'learner-friendly' teaching styles, and any other aspect of instruction that can bring about a positive affective response on the part of students.
- *Tech dynamics*: Using technology to its fullest potential in order to make certain learners find the kind of twenty-first-century learning environment they expect. It is at the centre of the pyramid because it is a powerful driving force in its own right, but it can also serve to enable and enhance the other dynamics that support the QLL Dynamics framework.

This framework applies to fully face-to-face (F2F), blended and virtual environments as well as learning experiences for children, teenagers and adults with different needs. It applies to English language learning, but it can apply to the teaching and learning of other languages as well.

At her April 2016 plenary for the 50th IATEFL Conference in Birmingham, England, Diane Larsen-Freeman referred to the need to part from traditional viewpoints and terminology in the field of SLA and look to more accurate conceptualizations of the teaching and learning process. In particular, she expressed a certain disagreement with the continued use of metaphoric terms such as 'input' and 'output' because they suggest – in her opinion – that students are to be seen as passive 'vessels' for L2 input and that output is only possible after language has been processed by what Chomsky has defined as their language acquisition device (LAD) or 'little black box'. Instead, she referred to 'the need to move on to beyond input-output metaphors to embrace a new way of understanding, one informed by Complexity Theory with its ecological orientation – one of affordances' (IATEFL, 2016, p. 2), specifically those of a 'first' and 'second' order. Based on Larsen-Freeman's exposition, *first-order affordances* could be defined as the elements and properties of the learning environment that facilitate or lead to language learning. *Second-order affordances* are the students' perceptions of and relationship with those elements and properties. In the end, she affirms that the understanding of and successful interaction between first- and second-order affordances can maximize the creation of opportunities for learning and learner engagement overall.

Why is this reference to affordances relevant to our discussion?

As I refer to the QLL Dynamics framework and in discussions throughout the volume, I use the terms 'input' and 'output' quite often. But I must point out that I do not make the mistake of using those terms along the lines of which Larsen-Freeman warns us not to. Rather, they are used in ways that consistently highlight the importance of having teachers and students enact a highly collaborative relationship in the classroom. In my understanding, 'input' is to be facilitated, crafted, selected and delivered in order to promote a proactive and protagonistic role for students as they engage in the learning experience. As for 'output', my contention is that opportunities are to be created for students to make the best use of their language resources and to express themselves with the greatest degree of personalization and creativity, which in turn should lead to both quantity and quality in spoken and written language. Of course, this also applies to virtual learning environments as well. In fact, the QLL Dynamics framework is

ACTIVITY

When you plan your next lesson, reflect on whether one or more of the dynamics can be applied at different times and with different content. Can you cover more than one of the dynamics at any given time?

perfectly amenable to Larsen-Freeman's conceptualizations of *affordances*. The four dynamics come to represent 'macro-affordances' of the first order, which the teacher and students can influence and enact directly for an optimization of the learning environment. The students' perception, response, motivation and performance in relation to the four dynamics come to represent the 'second order affordances' to which Larsen-Freeman refers. In sum, the QLL Dynamics framework is in line with both traditionalist and more current views of the second language acquisition (SLA) process.

Again, despite all of its promise, we must be certain technology is put to good use. Thornbury (n.d.) warns us that '[t]he power of technology is often enlisted in order to solve problems that are non-technological in nature, language learning being the prime example…. [T]he idea that change can be effected by a quick technological fix is ingenuous to say the least'. Similarly, Sharma and Barrett (2007) point out, 'It is important not to see teachers and technology as interchangeable and to clearly distinguish what one can do that the other cannot' (p. 13). In my opinion, rather than seeing technology as a generator of solutions in its own right, it should be seen as a tool, aid, or resource that can greatly facilitate the roles teachers and learners play in relation to those issues that are considered vital to successful learning. QLL Dynamics assigns such a role to technology, one that considers it an enabler, facilitator and an enhancer of student learning, not an all-powerful problem solver that works on its own. It is also important to remember that the implementation of technology does not necessarily have to be extensive in order to have a positive impact. A limited application of technology can also reap enormous benefits for teachers and learners alike. Here are some practical examples that illustrate the important role of technology in a QLL Dynamics class (Table 2.1):

Table 2.1 The Four Dynamics of the QLL Dynamics Framework and Respective Strategies (SLET)

Dynamic	Strategies for Learning Enhancement through Technology (SLET)
Kinaesthetic	Students are asked to come up to the interactive whiteboard (IWB) or monitor to highlight and explain the language samples that appear on the screen rather than simply say something while sitting down at their desks.
L2 Output	The teacher uses an entertaining, graphically attractive digital stopwatch to time oral participations as students engage in pair or group work activities, thus ensuring an equal amount of time to every student. The teacher can use a tablet to keep track of the students who have participated in class as well as samples of record speaking for assessment.
Motivating	The teacher decides to have students use their smartphones or tablets to look up and talk about the weather in their favourite cities around the world rather than use the course book's examples and activities on the same topic. In this case, the teacher wishes to do "something different" that students will appreciate.
Technology	The teacher uses the multimedia projector or large-screen monitor in class to show previously prepared examples of language rather than write them out on the board, saving time and maintaining learner engagement in the process.

ACTIVITY

For your next lesson, plan for a class that accounts for all of the dynamics according to the QLL framework. Video record it for self-assessment. What did you do to promote each one?

Face-to-Face (F2F) Implementation

Fully converting the classroom into a technology centre certainly requires an investment on the part of any educational institution. First, a reliable and capable Internet connection should be secured. Many software programmes, applications and videos on the Internet demand a broad bandwidth capability. If the connection is slow or intermittent, instruction can become less effective and the situation will cause frustration for the teacher and the learners as they wait for the content to stream. An Intranet connection can be equally valuable if there is a central server from which content, such as course-related audio and video, can be accessed quickly. In terms of equipment, there should be a PC or Mac in the classroom with a connection to a large-screen television, multimedia projector, or interactive whiteboard. The teacher must be able to use an agile, friendly interface for selecting content, taking attendance or accessing the Internet whenever needed. If possible, tablets and notebook computers for learners would be highly recommendable, but it is not a must; the same applies for teachers. Personal smartphones could be just as useful if the learners are old enough to have their own.

The multimedia language lab is an extension of the classroom experience and represents a vital space for additional language learning and practice. Over the years, a significant number of research studies have shown that computer use can provide engaging, stimulating input as well as opportunities for learning and practice that in many ways are just as effective as one-to-one tutoring, with a positive impact on learner attention span, language skill development, self-esteem and overall performance levels in a number of key areas (Meenakshi, 2013). In their review of over seventy studies on computer-supported language skill development, Liu, Moore, Graham and Lee (2002) cite the many findings that point to positive results in relation to grammar instruction and practice, writing, self-monitoring, reading, vocabulary development and levels of engagement with learning activities. Moreover, computer-mediated instruction has even been found to be helpful at the preschool level (Vernadakis, Avgerinos, Tsitskari and Zachopoulou, 2005). Therefore, determining the efficacy of computer-assisted language learning (**CALL**) as opposed to traditional teaching and learning is no longer a priority for research efforts (Beatty, 2013; Garrett, 2009). The research highlights the importance of the multimedia language lab in the language learning process because it is the place where learners can do focused work on computers during the school day or language centre session. Therefore, multimedia language labs are more than justified if they are well equipped and there is a purposeful plan that extends the learning experience beyond the main classroom.

From a past professional experience, I would like to refer to the idea of multimedia lab visits because they can promote greater awareness in learners as to the importance of using technology for learning. In their very first course, students were taken to the multimedia language lab as part of an induction process. The apps and websites were carefully chosen beforehand from among the wide range of resources available to the students through the institutional intranet. The idea was to familiarize them with the venue and make them aware of all of the virtues of CALL, especially the resources that the Institution was making available to them. The goal was to make the experience in the multimedia language lab as gratifying as possible, convincing them that it would be worthwhile exploring the rest of the content on their own and in their own time.

Ultimately, activities in the classroom and the computer lab were to be mutually supportive and lead to common learning goals, objectives and outcomes. These visits would be repeated at certain intervals later in the programme. More recently, at a growing language centre that was temporarily without significant technology in the classroom, students were taken to the lab to work with pre-installed videos and software (to deal with low bandwidth issues) as well as educational websites. Groups were scheduled to use the lab on a rotational basis per schedule and throughout the week.

To illustrate the role of the multimedia language lab, the following is a sample schedule for a highly intensive, 2200+ hour immersion-type programme I designed for a Latin American Ministry of Education. Its goal is to prepare hundreds of master's and doctorate level candidates to study abroad. It combines class time and multimedia language lab time, with the programme starting at a very low level of proficiency (e.g. A1 according to the CEFR). Figure 2.2 shows examples of daily schedules for different modules in the programme, with students working from 9:00 a.m. to 5:30 p.m. every day.

The programme has a general English curriculum, an academic English curriculum and a test preparation component, all of which flow together for an integrated, super-intensive immersion-like study programme. If a comparison were to be made to other educational models currently in use, it has some characteristics of both transitional bilingual education and sheltered immersion in the L2 (Krashen, 1996; Ray-Subramanian, 2011; Rossell, 2005). Essentially, all of the study time is face-to-face and on campus, with extensive online resources that are provided for additional practice in the multimedia language lab and outside of class. General language proficiency is developed first before students are asked to move on to highly specialized academic content. One distinguishing feature, however, is that specialized, academically oriented receptive skill development, often considered essential to success in academic settings (Christison and Krahnke, 1986; Genesee, Lindholm-Leary,

	Module 7	Technology	Module 11	Technology	Module 12	Technology
9:00 – 9:15	Intermediate 2: Unit 6A: Speaking, Writing, Reading, Listening, Speaking Strategy	Server-based audio & video; digital stopwatch for timing student turns and general activities, on-screen prompts and examples, etc.	Intermediate 10: Unit 11B: Reading, Grammar, Vocabulary Writing	Server-based audio & video; digital stopwatch for timing student turns and general activities, on-screen prompts and examples, etc.	Intermediate 12: Unit 6A: Vocabulary, Grammar, Speaking, Writing	Server-based audio & video; digital stopwatch for timing student turns and general activities, on-screen prompts and examples, etc.
9:15 – 9:30						
9:30 – 9:45						
9:45 – 10:00						
10:00 – 10:15						
10:15 – 10:30						
10:30 – 10:45	BREAK					
10:45 – 11:00	Pronunciation Practice	Pronunciation tips, examples and activities presented on the screen by teacher. More practice with tablets and smartphones using apps	Practice: Online Searches & Oral Reports	In the classroom, students will identify and discuss up to three topics of their interest. In the Computer lab; they will search for and later summarize the information related to one of the topics	English for Academic Purposes: Life Sciences & Robotics	In the computer lab, students work with Internet-based, online learning program especially designed for students at B2/C1 level of proficiency according to the Common European Framework (CEFR).
11:00 – 11:15						
11:15 – 11:30						
11:30 – 11:45						
11:45 – 12:00						
12:00 – 12:15						
12:15 – 12:30	BREAK					
12:30 – 12:45	Vocabulary & Fluency Practice	Combination of manual techniques, review of purpose for using GWL / NGSL, use of PowerPoint, digital flashcards on mobile devices, and digital learning logs	Learning Lab	Follow-up activities for practising the different language skills using the resources available in the lab. Using a wiki "live" to upload content resulting from student searches.	Introduction to TOEFL iBT: Practice	Online program with TOEFL iBT-informed exercises
12:45 – 13:00						
13:00 – 13:15						
13:15 – 13:30						
13:30 – 13:45						
13:45 – 14:00						

Figure 2.2 Sample schedule excerpts for a specialized programme that uses technology aimed at master's and doctorate students.

Saunders and Christian, 2005), is strongly reinforced from very early on in the programme and done concurrently with the general English component. Another important aspect of the programme is that there is a high degree of correlation between the activities in the classroom and those in the multimedia language lab, with substantial support from a variety of technological tools, resources and related strategies (SLET). In fact, the provision of massive amounts of general English and academic content/input, opportunities for language practice and means for self-assessment are all contingent upon technology. The programme's success, therefore, depends on a complex array of variables, including a successful application of the lessons learned in bilingual, ESL and immersion programes as well as a skilful use of technology from beginning to end.

In designing the programme and determining the role technology was to play in the pursuit of learning goals, a review of the literature on similar learning experiences was first conducted. In her overview of studies on L2 immersion programmes in French, Swain (1996) found that the amount of input, teaching strategies and styles, degree of immersion and age of entry were all preponderant factors in determining potential learner success. In most circumstances, learners were able to develop their writing skills to a high degree and offered rates of performance comparable to their L1 counterparts. However, the nature and amount of input obtained in class, most of which came from teachers, was oftentimes considered to be what she calls 'functionally restricted', leaving out important verb and other grammatical forms, or lacking the frequency of exposure and use that would normally be found in more authentic contexts. Additionally, L2 output came to represent a significant challenge, with most of it being categorized as minimal and not sustained in terms of length. Overall, the concluding hypothesis was that 'second language outcomes of the immersion approach can be enhanced through the provision of (1) focused input in problematic areas of grammar and vocabulary; (2) increased opportunities for the productive use of the target language in meaningful contexts; and (3) systematic and consistent feedback' (p. 98).

From a technological perspective, Swain's (1996) first point can be addressed by existing technologies, using commercially available software, such as Adobe Captivate. It is software that allows you to create exercises and other content for online learning. It can be used to present additional input related to forms, including aural and visual support, along with extensive use of online corpora and other sources of authentic, contextualized language, all of which is provided in this programme. For more L2 output opportunities, the QLL Dynamics pedagogical framework can be applied in the classroom to increase the quantity and quality of S–S and T–S interactions. Skype and other technological alternatives can be used for autonomous pair or group work outside of class. Feedback is provided in vast amounts in an automated format through a learning management system (LMS) or other technologies.

Upon closer scrutiny of the sample programme's schedule, we can see that the activities and tasks are much in line with what a twenty-first-century classroom learning experience can provide. In such an environment, the multimedia language lab has an important role as an extension of the classroom learning experience. Table 2.2 shows a sample learning activity scheduled for the lab, the pedagogic reasoning behind the use of technology, and the benefits one can expect for both teachers and students:

ACTIVITY

Make a list of resources and websites you would like to have your students use in the multimedia language lab. Have the necessary programmes installed. Then plan visits to the lab as part of a lesson. Survey your students afterwards to see what they thought of the experience.

Table 2.2 Activities and Technology for Highly Specialized Immersion-like Programme

Learning Activity	Pedagogical Rationale for Using Technology	Benefit for Teacher/Students
Students work with Internet-based, online learning programme for English for academic purposes (EAP) content.	Students are given access to a specialized learning management system (LMS) that provides them with abundant input/content related to their field of preference or area of expertise that would be unavailable otherwise.	Students can build up their vocabulary, apply grammar for EAP and develop their situational schema in relation to science-technology-engineering-maths (STEM) and other academic areas. The teacher is partly relieved of her/his duty in providing and explaining the highly specialized content.
Students identify 'EAP topics' of their interest, search for and later summarize the information related to one of the topics of their choice.	Students search for highly specialized content on the Internet. This affords them the opportunity to engage in practices that will be commonplace throughout the graduate and post-graduate study programmes in which they will eventually be participating.	The process of searching, reading, selecting and presenting information engages students in higher-order thinking skills. The presentation and dissertation stages promote high-quality L2 output.
Students use a wiki to upload content resulting from student searches.	Wikis are an ideal medium through which students can collaborate in providing course-relevant content for everyone's use. They are empowered to contribute and made to feel important.	Students personalize content and choose what they think is most relevant for the task at hand, promoting learner autonomy and self-determination.

Technology Standards

With the arrival of TESOL (Teachers of English to Speakers of Other Languages) Technology Standards and similar benchmarks, learners and teachers are now expected to demonstrate competencies and skills in the use of technology as they engage in the teaching and learning process. The immersion-like programme that has been presented as an example keeps this in mind. From the very beginning, learners are exposed to and asked to use a variety of technological tools and resources, and these include large-screen monitors, websites, mobile devices, graded videos and audio, commercial software, CD ROMS and others. As master's- or doctorate-level students, they will undoubtedly be asked to engage in research by using Internet-based databases, as well as offer presentations, read and listen to an extensive amount of academic content in the L2 and communicate frequently with their classmates or the professor by way of a range of electronic media. The instructors in the programme must also be sufficiently versed in the use of technology in order to ensure fruitful learning processes that will help these learners meet high standards in their future studies. In consequence, if we were to adapt the TESOL Technology Standards (Healey et al., 2011) and apply them to the students in this programme, or any other that adheres to a QLL Dynamics framework, we could say that they would be developing the following knowledge and skills for using technology:

- Demonstrate competency in the use of technology, including an ability to use a variety of technology tools, Internet browsers and input and output devices.
- Understand various communication conventions and protocols and how they differ across cultures, communities and contexts.
- Use and evaluate technology-based tools that promote or enhance productivity, skill building, communication, collaboration and research.
- Recognize the value of technology to support autonomy, lifelong learning, creativity, metacognition, collaboration, personal pursuits and productivity.

Technology and Planning

Despite the important contribution of international standards, an essential factor for making the implementation of technology a success is lesson planning, as it gives the entire learning experience a sense of direction and purpose. In relation to this, Jensen (2001) points out that, 'students come to class expecting their teachers to be prepared to teach. A lesson plan is part of that preparation' (p. 403). Harmer (2007) reminds us that lesson planning 'shows that the teacher has devoted time to thinking about the class.... For teachers, a plan gives the lesson a framework, and overall shape.... [T]hey need to have thought ahead, to have a destination which they want their students to reach, and some idea of how they are going to get there' (p. 156). In this regard, technology must play in important, clearly defined role in the learning process. Careful lesson planning ensures that technology will be used to full effect when it is called upon and appropriate to do so. Figure 2.3 shows a suggested planning sequence in which the role of technology is taken into account:

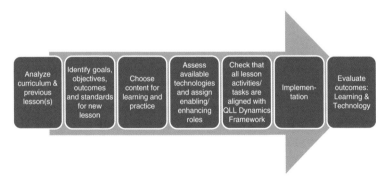

Figure 2.3 Technology planning process.

In this sequence, the potential role of technology is assessed. The teacher must review the learning path described in the lesson plan and determine whether the use of

ACTIVITY

Use the technology planning cycle for your next course. Devise a checklist and criteria to evaluate outcomes for learning and the effective use of technology. In the end, how did you and your students do?

technology at different moments will bring about better results for learning and practice or not. The *macro-variables of learner engagement* (e.g. *time, event codification* and *delivery*) come into play as does the overall QLL Dynamics instructional framework.

When speaking of a highly technological classroom that meets the expectations of today's twenty-first-century learner, we cannot fail to mention the use of e-books. At present, there are schools that have disposed of printed textbooks altogether, with students bringing their tablets and preloaded e-books to class, rather than the bulky, heavy-laden school bags of long-standing tradition. In support, there have been a few studies, particularly in higher education, that indicate a certain preference on the part of students for e-books over printed versions of course books, depending on the context (Rowlands et al., 2007). The general feeling in the field and other studies, however, seem to indicate the opposite: students will not choose the e-book option unless there are significant, highly recognizable advantages in terms of usability, interaction, functionality and overall added value. Indeed, research shows it may still be quite challenging for e-books to compete against printed course books (Huang, Lian and Cheng, 2012; Woody, Daniel and Baker, 2010). Consequently, mass-scale implementation of e-books in a wide variety of settings and contexts is probably still several years away.

ACTIVITY

Write your own teaching philosophy, or review it if you have one already. How do your everyday lessons reflect your philosophy when it comes to technology? Write a reflection.

Conclusion

In this chapter, we have discussed those essential elements that constitute or contribute to a technological classroom that serves to enhance overall learning. Specifically, among other considerations, there have been references to motivational factors; learner characteristics and expectations; philosophies on teaching and learning as well as pedagogical frameworks for classroom instruction; technical requirements, equipment and appropriate facilities; and actual examples of study programmes in which the classroom and computer language lab experiences are intertwined. In Chapter 3, we link the classroom learning experience to our learners' personal spaces and time, discovering ways in which a yet unexplored potential for language learning can be harvested.

Discussion Questions

1. What is the relationship between learner motivation and technology?
2. How does the QLL Dynamics framework promote maximum learner engagement and participation through technology? Could you think of three ways to apply it to your classes?
3. What are three ways in which technology can help make your work easier, saving time and effort?
4. Could you come up with examples of typical course book activities that could be replaced by more technologically enhanced lesson content?

5. How can you decide whether technology is required for a particular stage of your lesson? How can you assess the importance of the contribution after the lesson has concluded?

Suggested Readings

Egbert, J. and E. Hanson-Smith (2007). *CALL Environments: Research, Practice, and Critical Issues* (Alexandria, VA: TESOL International Association).
This book offers a vast collection of papers related to CALL, from a research and practical perspective.

Healey, D. et al. (2011) *TESOL Technology Standards: Description, Implementation, Integration* (TESOL International Association).
Guides teachers on how the learning environment can lead to technological proficiency on the part of teachers and students.

Mercado, L. A. (2012) *English Language Learning and Technology: Discovering a Whole New Potential* (Cengage Learning).
Provides teachers with an extensive array of ideas on how to convert the classroom into a technology-rich learning environment.

CHAPTER 3

Fostering Autonomous Learning

> *Autonomous learning is said to make learning more personal and focused and consequently to achieve better learning outcomes since learning is based on learner needs and preferences.*
>
> Nunan and Richards, 2015, xi

Historically, many have perceived second language acquisition and language proficiency development to be largely dependent on interactions in the classroom between teachers and students. Today, however, technology makes it more possible than ever before for language learners to 'explore and learn [the language] on their own outside of class, in their own free time', with a potential for learning that can transcend 'beyond what has been accomplished through more traditional educational paradigms' (Mercado, 2012a, p. 3). Thus, a successful twenty-first-century learning experience no longer depends solely on what can be accomplished in the classroom but also on what students can discover, learn and practise outside of a formal instructional setting. Project-based learning (**PBL**), for example, can be applied with technology to promote greater learner exposure to an enormous amount of L2 input. It can also create unique opportunities for learners to engage in new forms of L2 output and can foster the development of a variety of cooperative and autonomous learning strategies, among other benefits. The 'flipped classroom', a more recent pedagogical trend, seeks higher efficacy in the learning process by transferring instructional content and input in the language to the personal time and space of English language learners. This frees up time in the classroom so it can be more focused on productive interaction, feedback and the development of higher-order thinking skills. In light of these commanding trends, language teachers must acquire an expertise at using technology in order to create the conditions through which language learners can engage in successful autonomous learning, especially if we are to reach new milestones in the field. Some thoughts for reflection include:

- What is autonomous learning? How much of it should take place?
- How can I get my students to become autonomous learners, especially through technology?
- What learning modalities are amenable to autonomous learning?

Promoting Autonomous Learning

Teachers, curriculum planners, language programme administrators and e-learning providers must first have a clear understanding of what autonomous learning actually is, as it cannot take place if language learners are not ready for it. In defining autonomous learning, Holec (1996) defines 'self-directed', or autonomous, learning by referring to the learners' responsibility for taking decisions about the language they wish to acquire, how they wish to proceed in order to make it possible and how they assess and act on the results that come from these actions. Finch (2001) establishes a dividing line between 'autonomy [as] an *ability* that has to be acquired (learning how to learn) and… the learning that may take place when autonomy has been acquired' (p. 4). To succeed, he cites the need for language learners to acquire the knowledge and skills needed for the undertaking, the dispelling of preconceptions that favour a teacher-directed learning process, and the availability of time for dialogue between teachers and students about shared responsibilities for learning.

Teachers play a central role in preparing students by promoting open, ongoing dialogue that highlights the benefits, demands and strategies most associated with autonomous learning. They can provide invaluable insights to students on what to choose for independent study based on students' self-assessment of their own needs and preferences; how to study autonomously by employing a range of strategies; and when to study so that it fits in what may be a very busy personal schedule. Such discussions would also have to highlight the role of technology and how to make the best use of it. In order to carry out such an important role, teachers not only need to be well versed in the concept of autonomous learning but also on the technologies that are most compatible for promoting it. Nunan (2003) enumerates a nine-step, strategy-based programme that fosters learner autonomy, to which I have added the technological applications that are most likely to contribute to its success (Table 3.1).

Key stakeholders should come together and define an overall strategy for promoting autonomous learning. First, a needs analysis should be carried out, identifying what learners need and wish to learn. Such an effort should also establish a profile for the average student in terms of why this person is learning the language, how much time he or she is willing to commit to the endeavour outside of class, and the student's degree of proficiency in the use of technology. After the needs analysis, there should be a systematic review of the curricular content as well as the technological tools and resources that are available in order to determine how to best structure a programme that is conducive to self-directed study. Then learning events should be planned and structured for access outside the classroom. An induction process, which may vary in length depending on the characteristics of the group and the nature of the intended course plan, should be carried out at the very beginning of the learning process so learners are familiar with the content, how to access it and how they can best interpret outcomes along the way. Once learners are participating in the course, teachers should monitor their activity, progress and overall achievement, taking corrective measures in the classroom when

Table 3.1 Strategies for Fostering Autonomous Learning and Technology

Strategy	Technological application
Provide clear instructional goals, objectives and outcomes for learners.	Learning goals, objectives, outcomes and standards, or **LGOOS** (Mercado, 2015a), can be made available on the institutional intranet or even by e-mail or Facebook. There can also be a self-assessment for learners online that fosters awareness as to what they have learned.
Allow learners to create their own goals and content.	Learners can create their own presentations, videos, audios, images, publications, etc., and include references to LGOOS statements.
Encourage learners to use the L2 outside of the classroom.	Learners can read, listen, speak and write in English through a wide variety of communication media, learning resources and technological devices.
Raise awareness in learners in terms of how they learn.	Learners can keep an e-log and e-portfolio in order to reflect on their learning and determine the best practices and strategies for successful autonomous learning.
Encourage learner choice.	Learners can choose from titles in a virtual library of graded readers, diverse LMS alternatives and other web-based activities and tasks, learning targets, Internet-based project options, etc.
Encourage learners to become teachers.	Learners can create content so it can be explained or demonstrated to their classmates through role plays, presentations and lessons transmitted by e-media.
Encourage learners to become researchers.	Learners can research an endless number of topics in order to carry out project work, perform in class or simply pursue their own personal interests.

Source: Adapted from Nunan (2003)

ACTIVITY

Design an AL induction session for your next group of new students. What technologies will you focus on, and what are the key goals and objectives for their session?

necessary. Final course outcomes should be carefully reviewed and analysed to determine the degree of satisfaction and effectiveness of the autonomous learning component of the course.

At Euroidiomas, we recently conducted a Survey for Online Learners (SOL) among students in our 100 per cent online language courses in order to determine their needs and preferences, with most of the respondents ($n = 153$) being categorized as working adults between the ages of 20 and 49. These courses include live video sessions with online instructors. In relation to their needs and study habits, it was interesting to find the following:

- 80.8 per cent said they studied online because they had no time to study face-to-face in any modality or frequency.
- 50.8 per cent studied mainly in the mornings before going to work or class; 24.2 per cent studied mainly on weekends.
- 55.8 per cent studied less than two hours a day; 40 per cent studied two to four hours a day
- 90 per cent considered it necessary or very necessary to have an online tutor / instructor
- 97.5 per cent considered it necessary or very necessary to have an optional translation feature for the instructions or other content.

These results, although only referential in size and scope, provide important insights on learner needs, preferences and habits. The courses are all aimed at A1 to B1 level students, so the response regarding the translation feature is particularly relevant when considering low-proficiency students. The data on the amount of time can serve as a guide in designing or designating content in segments for study.

Virtues of Learner Autonomy

Autonomous learning is believed to contribute to higher levels of learner achievement, and this is a long-held belief not only in the field of second language acquisition but in general education as a whole. According to various studies, learners who are motivated in the classroom and who, in addition, purposefully engage in autonomous learning practices may very well demonstrate higher levels of competency and overall achievement as opposed to students who prefer to limit their learning to what may be covered in their regular classroom sessions (Dafei, 2007; Dickinson, 1995; Dincer, Yesilyurt and Takkac, 2012; Nunan, 2008). In fact, learners who engage in autonomous learning practices on their own accord apparently do so because their level of motivation and commitment to the learning process tend to be higher than what could be expected from other, less independent learners. Moreover, under certain conditions, learner autonomy can actually lead to increased motivation (Deci et al., 1991; Niemiec and Ryan, 2009; Spratt, Humphreys and Chan, 2002).

From the perspective of international standards and benchmarks, discerning the virtues of autonomous learning may not be so reliant on rigorous statistical analyses and extensive research, but rather on more commonsensical factors. For example, one could assume that the more time students devote to their English language studies, the greater the chance that they will learn more and the higher the level of proficiency they can achieve, other factors notwithstanding. Of course, teacher preparation and the quality of the course materials, curriculum, evaluation system, technology and facilities, among other variables, should all be working in favour of the learning process for time to have such an effect; otherwise, allotting more time to a study programme will not make much of difference, if any at all. Nevertheless, if a learner is willing to spend additional time outside of class studying and practising the language, any of the consequent learning could potentially serve to supplement the gains made in the classroom. Furthermore, such time could be specifically quantified and included among the study programme's hours in order to determine the learner's overall potential for proficiency development. Table 3.2, in which class contact hours are referentially aligned to target proficiency levels according to the Common European Framework of Reference to Languages (CEFR), is compared with Table 3.3, a summary of the hours in a blended learning programme alternative I designed for a Latin American Ministry of Education that targeted fourth- and fifth-year secondary students in its public school system:

Tables 3.2–3.3   Proficiency Levels and Blended Learning Alternatives

Required Class Contact Hours/ Face-to-Face Instruction	Target Proficiency Levels (CEFR)
180–200	A2
350–400	B1
500–600	B2
700–800	C1
1000–1200	C2

Source: Adapted from Mercado (2012b).

Aspect of the Programme	Proposed Characteristics
Class contact hours/ face-to-face instruction	Year 1: 24 weeks × 10 hours per week = 240 (late start in school year)
	Year 2: 36 weeks × 10 hours per week = 360
Online Learning Platform	Year 1: 24 weeks × 2 hours per week = 48 (late start in school year)
	Year 2: 36 weeks × 2 hours per week = 72
Total # of hours	720 face-to-face online
Target CEFR level	B2

In the comparison, we can see that the amount of face-to-face (F2F) instruction allotted to the high school English programme is already in the range of the minimum requirement for the target proficiency level, or B2 according to the CEFR. This is a low-risk scenario in which students are very likely to achieve their respective proficiency targets over two years.

Another blended learning solution I designed for the same Latin American Ministry of Education was aimed at improving the English language proficiency of close to 4000 teachers nationwide over the course of two years, after which they would go on to pursue studies in methodology (see Table 3.4). They would study in six-month, 24-session courses, with five hours of study and 45 minutes of break time in face-to-face sessions on weekends, and 80–100 hours of online study through an e-learning platform. Over a maximum period of two years, these teachers were to go from their starting level of proficiency to a B2. At the end of every level, they were required to take an

Table 3.4 Characteristics of a Blended Learning Programme for English Teachers

Aspect of the Programme	Proposed Characteristics
Class contact hours/ face-to-face instruction	Sessions were 5 hours every weekend for 24 weeks = 120 hours. There were four such courses going from A1 to B2 according to the CEFR.
Online learning platform	Total self-study time was approximately 4 to 4.5 hours a week = 80–100 hours. There were four levels, going from A1 to B2, according to the CEFR.
Total # of hours	200 hours minimum per course; 800 total hours for the programme
Target CEFR Level	B2 in two years

international proficiency examination to validate their progress and let them continue in the programme.

The programme came to a successful conclusion. Of the thousands of teachers, 98 per cent of them met or surpassed their proficiency targets according to the international proficiency examinations. A 96 per cent acceptance rate reflected the number of teachers who thought the programme was good or excellent. Finally, dropout or desertion rates were kept at a low 6 per cent, which was ideal considering that the target for the Ministry of Education was a maximum of 10 per cent. In this programme, the ratio of face-to-face to self-directed learning was kept at 60 per cent to 40 per cent at all levels. The Classroom and Autonomous Learning Integration, or CALI, concept (Mercado, 2015b) was applied in order to ensure student success; learners had to apply in the classroom what they had learned on their own, and they also had to successfully complete all of the e-learning assessments in order to pass the course, even though the class performances and tests were the only grades considered in the final average.

Based on these and other experiences, I would say that the factor that plays a key role in determining the achievability of desired proficiency targets in blended learning programmes is the ratio of class contact hours to the time designated for autonomous, or self-directed, learning. The greater the amount of time in favour of classroom instruction, the more likely it is for the learners to achieve their proficiency targets. 'Healthy' ratios of class contact to autonomous learning can be 70 per cent face-to-face/30 per cent online, 60/40 per cent, or even 50/50 per cent. However, actual figures will vary depending on the goals of the programme, the characteristics of the learners and the strength of the other variables that will have an influence on the outcomes (i.e. teacher proficiency, course materials, curriculum, etc.). The greater the ratio in favour of class contact time, the more of an 'insurance margin' there will be, which means the lower the risk of depending on e-learning resources that may not be fully up to the task. To increase the ratio in favour of online or virtual learning time, the learning management system and its respective content must be:

- truly robust, which means it should be fully comprehensive in terms of how well it covers the four skills and other aspects of the language;
- thorough in the number of opportunities for learning and practice as well as the amount of L2 input exposure;
- well-designed and substantiated pedagogically;
- accurate in its assessment and evaluation of learner progress and achievement; and
- informative in terms of the data the teacher (if there is one) and learners receive.

This last point is particularly important as learning analytics for English language learning, an emerging field, can provide abundant information on what is going well and what is not. Instruction and learning paths can then be adapted accordingly.

As a personal anecdote, a large Latin American university once requested a blended learning programme for its undergraduate students. When I asked them what the desired face-to-face/online ratio was, they said 80 per cent online/20 per cent face-to-face. The next logical question I had to ask was, 'What is the target proficiency level and what do you want them to be able to do when they have finished their studies?' Their answer was, 'We want them to reach a B2 level and to speak and write fluently in any academic setting!' I was then obliged to inform them that such a goal was incongruent with the ratio they desired. In the end, after some discussion, my proposal consisted of a programme that would go from a ratio of 50/50 per cent face-to-face to online, at the beginning, to 60/40 per cent and ultimately 70/30 per cent at the advanced level.

Expanding L2 Input

As stated earlier, the amount of time language learners are willing to commit to a study programme may determine the potential level of English language proficiency that is feasible for them to achieve. Nevertheless, despite all of the virtues of learning in the classroom – and the multimedia language lab as its extension – there may be aspects of the language learning process that may not be addressed sufficiently in a typical lesson due to time constraints, and exposure to L2 content is one of them. Again, time plays a very important role, as does the media through which L2 input is to be delivered. In addition, the scope of the input may seem limited, or 'functionally restricted' as Swain (1996) would describe it, at times due to the largely artificial nature of the classroom. The challenge is to make certain that conditions for input exposure and processing are fostered outside of the classroom as well, and in ways that allow the limitations in the classroom to be overcome.

Certainly, the fundamental role that L2 input plays in the second language acquisition process has long been established by research (Collentine, 2004; Gass and Selinker, 2010; Krashen, 1982, 2004). Krashen postulated his comprehensible input or i+1 hypothesis more than 30 years ago, and it stands fast in its acceptability to this very day. Yet, the processing of L2 input can be a highly intricate, complex affair to say the least, with additional implications for instruction. Schmidt's (1993) 'noticing hypothesis' sustains that for input to become intake, it must be attended and become noticed. It is a contention about learner awareness, both conscious and unconscious, that has been challenged over the years but nevertheless has been widely recognized as valid to account for many aspects of the second language acquisition process. Van Patten and Cadierno's (1993) framework for **process instruction** (PI) calls for exposure to input, input processing, accommodation and restructuring of the **interlanguage**, and eventually output. To achieve more effective input processing on the part of learners, PI advocates explicit grammar instruction with abundant input in the form of examples; information to students on how to best process such input; **structured input** in the form of activities that highlight form and meaning in the language; and feedback in its various forms (Morgan-Short and Bowden, 2006). In terms of exposure to language forms, Ellis's (2002) review of 11 studies on the role of **form-focused instruction** (FFI) in second language acquisition concludes that FFI can make a significant contribution to the language learner's development of implicit knowledge, depending on the target structure that has been chosen and the extent to which instruction is present. Overall, there is much in the research and literature that supports L2 input–oriented instruction. As a personal anecdote, my learning of Spanish was greatly aided by an extensive ongoing exposure to authentic input, especially after getting married to an L1 Spanish speaker and moving to a Spanish-speaking country. To this day, I have never taken a class to study Spanish.

In terms of accessibility, the potential for additional L2 input exposure outside of the classroom is boundless. Publishers, for example, offer course books for intensive English language programmes of all kinds and for students of all ages. As part of their offerings, it is now customary to include a variety of e-learning resources that can serve to provide additional L2 input to suit curricular needs. Yet, perhaps further diversity in the use of technological media for accessing content in the L2 should be sought. In relation, Van Patten and Cadierno's (1993) PI model applies in the autonomous learning realm as well. From a pedagogical perspective, the output stage would be expected to take place not only as language learners are following the autonomous learning path of their choice but also as a part of their subsequent performance in the classroom, which should reflect to a high degree what they were able to practise and learn on their own. In fact, this is perhaps one of the keys to successful autonomous learning: to transfer language skills and knowledge that were developed autonomously to performance-based learning situations in the classroom and ultimately to real life. From a classroom and autonomous learning integration (CALI) perspective (Mercado, 2015b), Table 3.5 refers to prerequisite conditions for second language acquisition according to Thornbury (2009), along with ways I believe technology can enhance learning in response to each one:

Table 3.5 Referential Associations between Conditions for SLA, Technology, and Teacher/Learner Enactment

Referential Condition	Role of Technology	Autonomous Learning Enactment	Classroom Learning Enactment
Input	The Internet can provide an endless amount of pedagogic and authentic L2 input.	Learners read or listen to graded texts through an LMS, Moodle or other online content platform. As an example of authentic input, they could go on a virtual tour of a famous museum, which would provide texts along with visual support.	Learners watch videos to practise a specific list of verbs in the past tense or watch a short video segment that stimulates discussion on the situation being depicted.
Data	Information about the language can be conveyed using a monitor, IWB, projection screen, tablet or smartphone.	Entire grammar, vocabulary, pronunciation, learning strategy and test preparation lessons can be made available for self-study.	Linguistically oriented information is made available on the screen for viewing, analysis and discussion.
Motivation	Students can use technological media that are familiar to them. Thus, they are likely to be proficient in their use and to prefer them to other, more traditional forms of content delivery.	By being in control as they choose their learning paths and receive vital ongoing information about their progress and achievement, the sense of empowerment and ultimate success can lead to higher motivation.	The learning environment becomes more amenable to learner schemata, needs and preferences. Technology introduces greater chances of novelty being present in the lesson.

Referential Condition	Role of Technology	Autonomous Learning Enactment	Classroom Learning Enactment
Feedback	Technology can provide automated feedback of all kinds to students, or facilitate the communication of asynchronous or synchronous teacher-generated feedback.	LMSs and other content-delivery systems can provide various types of automated feedback. They can also facilitate the provision of teacher-generated feedback.	After activities, tasks and exercises in class, correct answers or exemplars of target language can be shown on the screen for learner analysis and discussion.
Interaction and output	Technology can serve to provide the content learners need to engage in communicative interaction and stimulate target L2 output, perhaps more effectively than through other more traditional means.	Learners can interact with one another and produce the target language in either written or spoken form. Interactions can be synchronous or asynchronous, revealing the learners' authentic capacity for social interaction and effective communication, even without the guidance of a teacher.	In the classroom, teachers can use technology on their tablets or smartphones to gauge learner participation. With a variety of classroom and learner-owned devices, input and data can be delivered in order to stimulate L2 interaction and output.

ACTIVITY

Imagine you had to have your students do part of the course work, especially the learning of new material, at home. What activities and tasks would you assign? Go through your course book and decide on which activities you would cover in class and which ones your students would have to do at home. What's the ratio?

An excellent example of autonomous learning is the US Department of State's *Trace Effects*, a 'collaborative English language video game experience for students ages 12–16' (US Department of State, n.d.). Much like *Second Life*, it provides an interactive virtual world in which students can hone their language skills and learn about American culture through puzzles, games and adventures. I have used it as an important resource supporting the creation of virtual learning experiences, getting an enthusiastic response from students. It is free and represents pedagogically oriented gamification at its best. It can be accessed at http://americanenglish.state.gov/trace-effects.

Learning Modalities

One form of autonomous learning whose innate characteristics promote many of the principles, concepts and insights presented in the previous sections of this chapter is *project-based learning*, or PBL. It is a pedagogical model for learning whose foci in the SLA field have expanded over the years. They have gone from providing learners with opportunities to receive comprehensible input, produce comprehensible output and recycle language skills to serving as a means of facilitating cooperative learning, content-based and ESP instruction, higher-order thinking skills and technology-supported project work in general (Beckett, 2006). PBL can be highly challenging, motivating and empowering for learners. It can serve as a perfect vehicle that promotes the development of language skills with a high degree of success, as well as responsibility for the learners' own learning and work (Stoller, 2002).

Although most of the research related to the effectiveness of PBL has been focused on subject areas that are encompassed within the field of general education, many of the findings can be extrapolated to apply to SLA because of the cognitive, affective and instrumental variables they share. In his review of PBL-centred research studies, Thomas (2000) found that the studies were mainly concentrated on the overall effectiveness of PBL, formative aspects of PBL implementation, associations between learner characteristics and the effectiveness of PBL, and the testing of a specific aspect or feature of PBL. With some results that were dramatic and others whose results can be open to debate, in general it could be surmised that 'PBL seems to be equivalent or slightly better than other models of instruction for producing gains in general academic achievement' (p. 34). There were notable improvements in the development of higher-order and problem-solving skills in learners, as well as a highly positive affective response from both learners and teachers. In a more recent survey of PBL-centred research, Bell (2010) cites positive results in terms of learner achievement, the acquisition of 'real-world' life skills and learner affect, with a special supporting role reserved for technology in all phases of PBL.

For project-based initiatives to succeed, they must meet certain requirements. They should engage learners in a problem that requires resolution, with enough information and resources to get them started on the task. Learners should also be provided the orientation and means to find additional information and resources needed to carry out the task to completion. Although projects can be done on an individual or group basis, the latter scheme promotes cooperative learning, affording learners the opportunity to combine their strengths and make up for their individual limitations. Of course, the theme, topic and actual activities and tasks that make up the project should all be engaging, relevant and meaningful. Moreover, projects should be achievable, not overly complex, and designed in a way that promotes an equal amount of participation and effort on the part of each member of the team, if it is a group endeavour. Finally, whenever possible, teachers should provide feedback and guidance as learners work on their projects, giving them just enough information to keep them on track. Here is a checklist of what project design on the part of the teacher should involve:

1. Decide on the variability of topics and themes in relation to the number of project alternatives. Students should be given a choice whenever possible.
2. Decide on the time frame and stages (if any).
3. Identify the nature and aims for the project, or each of the projects, as well as their components. They should all be related to course content and learning goals, objectives, outcomes and standards, LGOOS (Mercado, 2015a).
4. Determine the role of technology.
5. Create the content (e.g. information, graphic or visual support, resources, etc.) for the project or each of the projects.
6. Create the documentation that will present the project or choices as well as the respective instructions and other important information. It can be in printed and e-form.

As an example, I created a *CLIL* WebQuest some years ago called 'Life in Space'. Students were asked to get into groups and imagine they were going on a trip to a distant planet or moon of their choosing. The project was divided into five stages: (i) 'Planning', or a description of the arrangements made for the trip and the events surrounding their departure; (ii) 'The Way There', or the actual trip in space; (iii) 'Landing', or their coming out of hyper-sleep and landing on the planet or moon; (iv) 'The Problem', which was a problem I presented to them for resolution midway through the project; (v) and the

ACTIVITY

Find a website for creating a WebQuest. Using the guidelines and the example above, create a project for your class. They can access the site from home or the multimedia language lab. At the end, survey your students and ask them how they benefitted from the experience.

conclusion. Each student was asked to write about each stage of the 'mission', and later, as a group, they presented the details surrounding their trip. A PowerPoint presentation was optional but provided a way of further distinguishing levels of performance among the group members. The project served as a means of getting them to practise their listening, speaking, reading and writing skills, as well as expand their vocabulary, grammar and even pronunciation. It engaged them in research, as they had to find information on planets and moons, spacecraft, cryogenic suspension, nourishment in space and other details that would have to be included in their narrations. The problem-solving component was meant to enhance their higher-order thinking skills, and the teamwork promoted collaborative learning. To improve their chances of success, I gave them information and feedback along the way, as needed. The project can still be found today at http://teacherweb.com/PE/ICPNA/LifeinSpace/index.aspx.

Flipped learning is a more current pedagogical trend in the field of English language teaching and learning than PBL. However, it is not so new in other educational fields, especially at the secondary and higher education levels. Its virtues are many. In Bishop and Verleger's (2013) survey of 24 studies in higher education addressing flipped classrooms, the findings were found to be largely positive. Specifically, they found the following: (i) student perceptions generally favoured in-person lectures to video lectures, but preferred interactive classroom activities over lectures; (ii) there was some evidence suggesting that learner performance could improve under certain conditions in a flipped-classroom modality of learning; (iii) learners who watched video lectures tended to be better prepared for in-class activities than those who were given textbook readings; and (iv) shorter rather than longer videos were preferred by learners. In Herreid and Schiller's (2013) own survey of research studies on flipped learning, specifically applied in the area of science, technology, engineering and maths (STEM), the findings were very similar, with learner satisfaction rates and performance being generally higher than what could be found in more traditional classrooms; learners were also more open to cooperative learning and innovative teaching methods. In Hamdan et al.'s (2013) review of the literature and research on flipped learning, they cite a number of studies in K–12 and higher education, with learners generally exhibiting higher levels of engagement with the course, collaboration in helping their classmates, discipline in class and, most importantly, better performance on achievement tests and other assessments.

Research on flipped learning as it is applied to English language teaching and learning is somewhat scarce. However, in an exploratory study of a more anecdotal nature, Han (2015) used the flipped classroom approach to work with a group of advanced level students. The positive effects included a higher degree of motivation, expanded opportunities for learning outside of class and greater learner autonomy. Nevertheless, the teacher spent just as much time preparing lessons as he would have in a traditional classroom, pointing out that 'teaching the same course every semester requires an initial investment of time and effort, since the content can be recycled with slight modifications, gradually lightening the workload. Teaching a different level each semester, however, presents a significant challenge for the instructor' (p. 106).

In general, we can conclude that 'flipped learning' has positive effects on learners depending on the context and conditions in which it is being realized. Again, as Berrett (2012) points out, with a flipped classroom approach 'Students cannot passively receive material in class.... Instead they gather the information largely outside of class, by reading, watching recorded lectures, or listening to podcasts... And when they are in class, students do what is typically thought to be homework, solving problems with their professors or peers, and applying what they learn to new contexts.' (p. 1). From a language learning perspective, this means that learners are exposed to pedagogical and other comprehensible L2 input that would normally be provided, discussed and acted on in class, such as grammar and vocabulary lessons, reading and listening to texts, lectures, authenticated (i.e. graded, simulated 'real-life') and authentic videos and so on. With the time that is freed up in the classroom, learners can focus on activities and tasks that foment varied types of interaction in the L2 for communication practice, the development of higher-order thinking skills, corrective and other forms of feedback, and collaborative learning, among other benefits. Rather than introduce L2 content for the first time, the teacher can elaborate on, clarify and channel such information for learners to consolidate their understanding as well as their ability to apply what they have learned to real-life situations.

One of the challenges associated with applying flipped learning is that students are required to set aside part of their personal time and space in order to engage in L2 content review, processing and practice. This implies a high degree of discipline on the part of learners if the delivery of content is systematic, abundant and a strong determiner of what is to be covered later on in class. As stated earlier, the teacher is also required to take a significant amount of time to prepare the materials and exercises for self-directed study on the part of the learners, especially if a course is being taught for the first time. In order to facilitate learner engagement with L2 content for flipped classrooms, teachers, curriculum planners, language programme administrators and e-learning providers should make certain that it is:

- engaging and meaningful;
- course- or proficiency-level appropriate;
- not excessively complex or information-laden;
- delivered in short, manageable segments;
- clearly focused on target language forms and topics; and
- linked to classroom activities, tasks and even grades.

As an example, let us assume that there is a lesson coming up on how to express wishes, using *I wish + were/would/could*. First, the presentation would have to be created using an application that features the ability to insert audios, videos, voices, music, and other media. PowerPoint Mix (enhanced PowerPoint for editing), Mozilla Popcorn Maker (video editing), Aximedia Soft's (no TM logo) Slide Show Creator (photo and music editing) and others can help teachers create highly dynamic presentations, slide shows and other media for presentations. The language lesson on 'wishes' could include a short video clip of the teacher explaining the topic, the 'grammatical formula' to show the form, contextualized examples shedding light on the form's meaning and use, and one or more videos showing how the language is used in real life, using DiVii or a similar website/application. The task can have students search for more examples on their own by using the Internet or an actual site like Brigham Young University's COCA corpus. Finally, students should read the activity and task descriptions for the following day's lesson, which will tell them what they will be expected to do in class and why. The activities and tasks may include group work on devising explanations of the grammar (i.e. *wishes*), role plays and a writing activity in which they send a real e-mail to someone describing a wish they have, among other alternatives.

ACTIVITY

Instead of teaching a specific grammar, vocabulary or pronunciation point in class, with a regular course book, use a laptop and record yourself teaching it from home. You can insert the video in a PowerPoint presentation and include examples on various slides. Post it on a blog for your students to access. Try to keep it to a maximum of four or five minutes.

As an example, I created a flipped **content-based learning (CBL)** course aimed at Advanced B2+/C1 level learners who were required to take CLIL courses in management as part of a special language learning programme. The challenges included (i) creating the right amount of content so it would not be too taxing on learners' free time; (ii) creating classroom tasks and activities that would not be entirely dependent on independent work; and (iii) finding content that was highly comprehensible. Regarding the search for content, the course led to short videos, articles and other texts that were delivered in manageable chunks. These were made available on the institutional intranet. Classroom activities were designed so that they would 'teach' the lesson point simply by having learners do them. (For example, by completing a Gantt/project schedule chart in class, learners would be able to understand what it was for and how to fill one out, even if they hadn't watched the video or read the text the night before; if they had, they would only strengthen their understanding by doing the task.) The final outcome has been more than satisfactory. Taking into consideration several updates from new editions of the course books, students are still working with basically the same activities and tasks to this day and enjoying them. There is also a very high degree of teacher satisfaction with the course content and less workload because the tasks are reusable.

Conclusion

In this chapter, we have come to appreciate the importance of autonomous learning and how it can expand the learning envelope beyond the constraints that are inherent in traditional, classroom-centred educational paradigms. Undoubtedly, autonomous learning harnesses a yet unexplored potential for learning that could establish new thresholds in the future. With technology, there is no limit as to what learners can achieve; they can learn what, when, where and how they want, making 24/7 learning much more than what many would consider a simple cliché. What is essential, however, is for there to be a high degree of classroom and autonomous learning integration (CALI) (Mercado, 2015b) so they can truly complement each other for optimal learner performance and achievement. Only then can we be certain as to whether our students really took advantage of the time they worked on their own and to what extent that has advanced their development in the language.

Discussion Questions

1. What are some advantages of using a commercially available e-learning platform or learning management system to promote autonomous learning?
2. Is there an ideal class time/autonomous learning time ratio for blended learning study programmes? What would you suggest for a group of busy executives? For an entire programme for university students?
3. In your opinion, what are the three most important conditions from David Nunan's strategy-based programme for fostering autonomous learning? How would you apply technology to advance each of them in your own setting?
4. What types of classroom learning and autonomous learning would you say are completely interchangeable?

5. What are some similarities and differences between PBL and flipped learning? Which would you prefer for a very elementary-level English course? Why?

Suggested Readings

Beckett, G. H. and P. C. Miller (2006) *Project-based Second and Foreign Language Education: Past, Present, and Future* (Charlotte, NC: Information Age Publishing).
Offers an extensive look at project-based learning from both a theoretical and a practical perspective.

Bergmann, J. and A. Samms (2014) *Flipped Learning: A Gateway to Student Achievement.* (Arlington, VA: International Society for Technology in Education).
Offers invaluable insights on 'flipped learning', a trend that is emerging in ELT.

Nunan, D. and J. C. Richards (2015) *Language Learning beyond the Classroom* (New York: Routledge).
Presents 28 case studies of autonomous learning experiences at the institutional and individual classroom level.

4 Curricular Vetting for Online and Mobile Learning

> *Content selection is an important component of a learner-centered curriculum. In such a curriculum clear criteria for content selection give guidance on the selection of materials and learning activities and assist in assessment and evaluation*
>
> Nunan, 1988, p. 5

Today, the variety of educational resources available for online and mobile-assisted language learning (**MALL**) can seem endless. From podcast lectures, learning management systems (LMSs) and massive open online courses (**MOOCs**) to **HTML-5**-based software and apps, language corpora, Prezi presentations and YouTube videos, teachers have a wide range of alternatives to choose from. Yet, considering the complexity of the language learning process and the lessons learned in previous chapters, determining which resources are most likely to make a significant contribution may not be such an easy task. Examining the possibilities, certain questions arise:

- What is quality language learning?
- In view of all of the abundance, what should teachers prioritize when integrating tech resources with classroom instruction?
- How can teachers, curriculum planners and language programme administrators vet these resources to make certain they can serve a useful purpose towards the advancement of language learning?

In order to answer these and other questions, perhaps we must first look at the essentials of curriculum design, planning and assessment, particularly those principles and concepts that are most supportive of quality, technology-rich learning environments.

Quality Standards

Curricular vetting (Mercado, 2012b) is a process by which contents (e.g. L2 input, exercises, activities, audios, videos, etc.) are reviewed, evaluated and primed for inclusion in a curriculum. It is a multilayered approach that seeks to ensure quality learning experiences. These can take place either in a classroom setting or when language learners continue to process, learn and practice the L2 on their own. Applied to technology-based learning resources, it can make the difference between aimless, redundant content creation and purposeful curricular design that is more likely to lead to discernable outcomes in language development. According to Mercado (2013b), 'there is a need for ... applications – whether they are teacher-created, free online resources, or commercial products – to go through a vetting process, particularly during the development or pre-selection stage.... This would address to a significant extent the issues of pedagogical credibility as well as the measurability of outcomes' (p.1). But what is quality learning? I propose the following formulaic depiction of what maximizing quality in a language study programme entails (Figure 4.1):

Figure 4.1 Formulaic depiction of study programme quality.

Adapted from Mercado (2012b).

In other words, in order to maximize quality in a curriculum or study programme, one must:

- L (A:P): Maximize the learning (L) that is to take place, whether it is actual (A) or perceived (P). The first refers to the type and amount of learning that can be objectively measured and compared to officially established criteria for learner achievement. The second is what language learners believe they are learning based on their own perceptions.
- SS (PA:V:FE): Maximize stakeholder satisfaction (SS) as it is expressed through personal affect, value and the fulfilment of expectations. Personal affect (PA) is how well language learners feel as they are engaged in the learning process, and as a result it has a direct impact on their motivation to continue with their studies. Value (V) is what learners are offered in return for their investment in terms of time, effort and money; the higher the perceived value or the more the get, the more likely it is that learners will associate the curriculum or study programme with a quality offering. The fulfilment of expectations (FE) is in relation to what learners feel about the teachers' degree of preparation, study materials, facilities, technology, support and customer services, ambiance, study schedules and convenience, among other factors.
- T: The maximization of all of the other variables (i.e. L/SS) must take place within a certain period of time, which can be the length of a lesson, course, instructional level and, ultimately, the entire programme.

Certainly, teachers, e-learning platforms and the study programmes they sustain are evaluated each and every day, and the main goal is to ensure that learners will want to continue their studies and then return for the next course or module. With *curricular vetting* of e-resources, there are some general considerations to keep in mind:

- There should be a clear purpose for the L2 input, exercise, task, activity or project in relation to the learning goals for the course.
- It should help language learners with a specific language skill or feature that they want to develop on their own. The interface

and presentation of the content should be user-friendly, self-explanatory, and aesthetically attractive.

- Whenever possible, it should allow for personalization, whether it is in the choice of the background colour, the ability to insert a picture as wallpaper, the option of changing the fonts or even the order of the content according to personal preference and need.
- Anything language learners are asked to do on their own should be meaningful, relevant and engaging, with feedback that gives them a clear indication as to how much progress they are making.
- The content should not be overwhelming in terms of the amount that is made available or how it is presented.
- Reiteration and recycling of content are important for purposes of learning consolidation as is the availability of sample models of the language that cater to diverse genre in support of the language skill in question.
- Accessibility should be simple, and the application or software should be reliable, which, simply speaking, means it should work at all times. Ideally, the content should allow for a follow-up in the classroom.
- Anything that is learned should be applicable to the 'real world'.

Among the key considerations for any Internet-based or mobile-assisted language learning (MALL) content is the amount, form and purpose of L2 input. Here are some key criteria to consider:

- *Target form(s)*: What grammar, vocabulary, pronunciation or other language feature do we wish to cover?
- *Course/proficiency level*: Is the content comprehensible, taking into consideration the learners' course or proficiency level?
- *Quantity and length*: How much content do we want to deliver, and how long should each exposure be, considering the learners' processing capabilities?
- *Scope*: How extensive do we want to be with the examples so that learners can fully comprehend how the form is used and how it should be produced?
- *L2 output prompts*: Do we want to include prompts at some point that will encourage learners to use the language productively (e.g. speaking or writing) as a means of confirming processing, comprehension and transfer?

- *Curriculum correlation*: Is the content aligned with the curriculum, specifically course or programme goals, objectives, outcomes and standards?
- *Buy-in*: Is the L2 input presented in a way that will ensure learner engagement through the learning, practice and output (if present) cycle?

As an example of vetting a MALL activity to make certain it is likely to be effective, the following example is a contribution from Yina Vasquez and Nelson Jaramillo, two teachers who work at the Centro Cultural Colombo Americano, a binational centre in Cali, Colombia, that does much to promote technology among its faculty. The name of the activity is *Comic Strip* and the goal is to motivate students to talk using adjectives and other target vocabulary while developing fluency. It can be used at any course or proficiency level. To carry it out, Yina and Nelson advise the following:

1. Teacher shows students some common comic strips, using a television or projector.
2. Then teacher shows students a comic strip created with real photos and asks students to come up with the story behind it.
3. Students are asked to work in groups of three and to use their own smartphones or gadget to take the pictures (minimum of four) they need to create their own comic strip.
4. Students are asked to switch their smartphones or gadget with another group. Then, they are to come up with the story behind their partners' pictures.
5. Students are asked to compare their story to the real story.
6. Teachers can find templates at the following website: http://www. makebeliefscomix.com/Printables/print.php?category=Blank_ Comix_Templates&file=1_Print.GIF.

In the example above, the teacher is seeking 'buy-in' by making the activity highly engaging, collaborative and novel. The target language is clearly identified, as is the purpose of the activity. It is situational because students can go around the building or the neighbourhood to take pictures, consolidating

ACTIVITY

Evaluate the content of your next technologically supported lesson, whether it is grammar, vocabulary, reading or another form of input. Use the above criteria for L2 input. In your opinion, which three are the most important? Does your lesson meet all of the criteria?

their learning of the target language as they interact with the environment around them. Applying the vetting criteria, it would seem this activity is largely compliant.

Bloom's Taxonomy

A broader, more systematic way to vet online and MALL content is to use Bloom's Taxonomy for the Cognitive Domain or the Revised Bloom's Taxonomy, also called the RBT (Anderson et al., 2001). Whether the focus is on reading, listening, speaking, writing or some other aspect of the language, learners should be encouraged to move up the taxonomy's scale of cognitive complexity as they progress through a study programme. Research on the applicability of Bloom's Taxonomy has long established that the higher the cognitive demands on learners that come from the teacher's questioning behaviour and tasks or activities, the greater the chances of achieving higher levels of learner performance and achievement (Gall, 1970; Redfield and Waldman Rousseau, 1981; Zohar and Doli, 2003). Consequently, English language learning study programmes that are accessed by way of online learning platforms and MALL alternatives should integrate critical and higher-order thinking throughout their curricula. The essential principle is that the higher the course or proficiency level, the greater the number of opportunities that learners should have to engage in higher-order thinking skills.

Research has found that applying Bloom's Taxonomy to curricular development and implementation generally leads to positive results. In a study by Noble (2004), 16 teachers with learners from kindergarten through Grade 6 worked over 18 months with a multiple intelligences (MI) and RBT matrix in order to plan their lessons. Among the results, the 'teachers reported consistently that the typologies of MI theory and RBT helped them cater to the individual learning capabilities of the students in their classes and thereby facilitated student success' (p. 198). This suggests that Bloom's Taxonomy or the RBT can be used not only to assess the quality of specific content but also to provide various levels of L2 input and activity/task types for the same class or group, serving as a form of scaffolding for weaker students. Thus, those that are stronger or gifted will engage the higher level prompts while the weaker students can do the lower level alternatives, all with the same learning goals and objectives. As another example, in a review I conducted of 72 activities distributed among six chapters in what was supposed to be a higher intermediate-level course book (Mercado, 2012b), only 15 per cent of the activities actually engaged students in critical thinking (e.g. analysis, evaluation and synthesis). Because international language standards and guidelines, such as ACTFL, can make a strong association between critical thinking and proficiency level as a criterion for compliance, using content that does not foster higher-order thinking in learners can inhibit true progress in proficiency development. Needless to say, the book was not chosen or even used in a pilot study.

In general, for the analysis of each component of an L2 prompt, exercise, activity or task, the reviewer should determine the highest level of cognitive processing in which learners must engage. For the most part, that is the peak by which the learning opportunity will be judged. Perhaps the simplest way to vet content is to make a list of all of the actions learners will be expected to carry out as they engage in a task or activity, which could be translated into a list of verbs. This list should be compared to the verbs commonly associated with the different levels of Bloom's Taxonomy, to analyse the complexity of the cognitive processes demanded from learners as they perform.

To illustrate, here is a sample list of questions that could be formulated as prompts for online, interactive speaking practice sessions between teachers and students. The questions increase in complexity according to Bloom's Taxonomy and RBT:

What can you tell me about the 1980s?

Think about it for a minute.

- Name three important events that happened in the 1980s. (*Knowledge/Remembering*)
- What was the music in the 1980s like? (*Comprehension/ Understanding*)
- Which song do you remember most from that era and why? (*Application/Applying*)
- Why would someone create this sticker in the first place? (*Analysis/Analysing*)
- Compare the 1980s with the present. Was the music then better? Why or why not? (*Evaluation/Evaluating*)

ACTIVITY

Analyse the activity or task you have assigned for homework. Are you asking your students to engage in higher-order thinking? If not, how could you modify the questions or prompts to make the assignment more cognitively challenging?

- Describe something that could have happened differently in the 1980s. How could it have changed the history of your country? (*Synthesis/Creating*)

The prompts and question samples above show the relative ease with which language learners can be asked to engage in all of the levels of cognitive processing according to Bloom's Taxonomy. Regarding Noble's (2004) study, the weaker students would start off with the lower-level questions and work their way to the critical thinking questions over time, with support and guidance. This is an arrangement that is particularly amenable to e-learning environments, especially those that are computer adaptive (e.g. the difficulty level of the questions adapts progressively to learner responses) in nature. Of course, the prompts and questions would have to undergo other vetting criteria as well (e.g. format, the topic's level of engagement, etc.), but they can suit their purpose if delivered at the right time within the online study programme or in a format that is compact enough for MALL.

As a case study example, Euroidiomas is a language centre in Lima, Peru, that has live teacher–student interactions by way of Moodle video conferencing as part of its 100 per cent online learning programme (Skype was used previously). Figure 4.2 depicts one of several preparatory slides that is supposed to prepare students for their live, online interaction with their teacher later in the week. The topic is healthy foods and eating. The questions are all ranked according to Bloom's Taxonomy, beginning with *knowledge* and continuing through *evaluation* and *synthesis*.

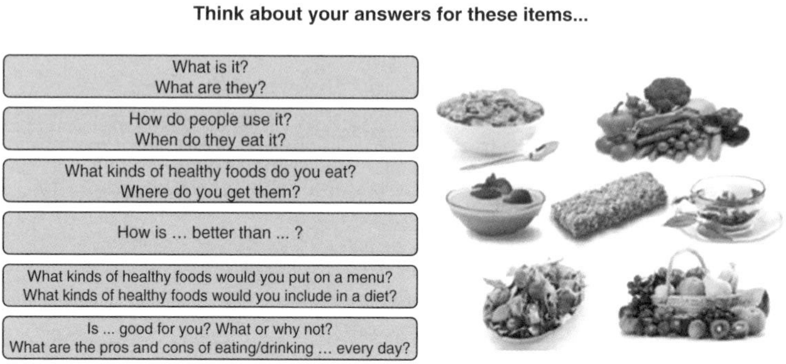

Think about your answers for these items...

What is it?
What are they?

How do people use it?
When do they eat it?

What kinds of healthy foods do you eat?
Where do you get them?

How is ... better than ... ?

What kinds of healthy foods would you put on a menu?
What kinds of healthy foods would you include in a diet?

Is ... good for you? What or why not?
What are the pros and cons of eating/drinking ... every day?

Figure 4.2 Slide from *Let's Speak* preparatory material for video sessions with online tutors.

Authenticity

The authenticity of the language learning process has long been an issue in the field and one that should be taken into consideration as an additional criterion when vetting content for online and MALL learning. In her review of the literature and research, Tatsuki (2006) identifies the authenticity of language learning opportunities and events as divided into three main categories: authenticity of language (e.g. L2 input for learners and the learners' own interpretation of the data); authenticity of the activities and tasks aimed at promoting language learning, which refers to how closely they resemble 'real-life' situations; and the authenticity of the social interactions and relationships within the language classroom. For the purpose of our discussion, we focus primarily on the first two, as they are the ones that most apply to autonomous learning through online and MALL alternatives. As for the relationship between authenticity and autonomy, Mishan (2005) points out:

> In the language learning context, autonomy and authenticity are essentially symbiotic. The 'ideal', effective autonomous learner

will utilize a wide variety of authentic sources in his/her learning and it is in an autonomous learning environment that such texts can best be explored. Case studies on learner-experiences in self-instruction, for example, have found that particularly at higher proficiency levels, learners benefit from interacting with authentic texts in autonomous modes. Conversely, authenticity fosters autonomy.' (p. 9)

Certainly, the notion that authenticity fosters autonomy is a crucial one. However, I would add that there must be some form of initial scaffolding and support from the teacher in order to make certain that learners will not get lost in 'a sea of authenticity'. This can be done by providing ample information on what to find initially and where to find it, as well as by giving recommendations to learners on how they can then search for their own content. Again, there must be a high degree of correspondence between what learners do and explore on their own and what is being done in the classroom, at least initially, in order to maximize results. By carefully selecting L2 input and designing appropriate activities or tasks, learners will stay focused on what they need to learn. With some explicit training on learning strategies, learners will have the means to make the best out of their autonomous learning ventures.

Because of its portability, MALL is an excellent medium that can bring learners close to authentic situations and input in the language. Many new technologies for mobile devices are now capable of facilitating the application of *situated learning*, a concept that upholds the belief that 'learning which takes place in a particular language context is more effective than studying similar content in the classroom' (Beatty, 2013, p. 4). More specifically, situated learning takes place as learners interact outside of a formal instructional setting with other English speakers or the English-speaking environment in which they may happen to find themselves, making it more meaningful and memorable. As Beatty explains, situated learning may have language learners access a set of previously identified expressions or a map on their mobile phone as they prepare to engage native speakers on the street in order to ask for directions. He goes on to point out that mobile devices in particular have the potential to serve as pedagogical tools outside the classroom in support of situated learning because they can store or wirelessly access a variety of media (e.g. text, images, sound and video) for later reference. Therefore, situated learning through technology has a great potential for complementing more-structured learning experiences.

Despite the potential benefits of situated learning, there are some challenges as well. In an EFL context, where exposure to L2 input can be extremely limited outside of a classroom setting, the probability of learners encountering native speakers of the language and engaging them for anything other than minimal communication can be very low. Therefore, language teachers can promote other kinds of situated learning opportunities for their students by having them experience L2 input very much like they normally would in a 'real-life' situation using the L1 in their own countries. Perhaps the easiest way for them to do that initially is by having them take advantage of well-known mobile apps they are accustomed to using on a daily basis, but changing the configuration so the language is English. This can be particularly helpful for learners with lower levels of proficiency because the scope of the language on apps is narrower and usually delivered in small, manageable chunks. Here are some examples from among a potentially limitless variety of options that could be used:

- *Waze/Google maps*: The first app finds the easiest routes to get you to your destination by car or walking. Someone speaks to you as you move along the suggested route, telling you where to turn, the distance to the next turning point, the amount of traffic ahead, the location of accidents, and even whether the police are nearby. The text and voice can be in English. The second app is more of a GPS, with instructions in English. The only limitation in both cases is that the pronunciation of the local street names may seem unusual or somewhat difficult to make out.

- *CityMaps2Go*: This app provides you with a map of the city you are in and extensive information on a wide variety of locations that may be of interest to the user, including hotels, restaurants, bars, and so on.
- *EasyTaxi/Uber*: This app allows you to call a cab and have it arrive within five minutes. The information can be switched to English, so learners can become thoroughly familiar with the app's language in a short period of time.
- *Trello*: This app helps you organize your daily activities, and it can include other members, including several students who may want to work together as a group.
- *Social Media*: Facebook, Instagram, LinkedIn and other social media can be configured to English. Since they are used so often, learners may be able to acquire vocabulary associated with interaction, access, help, and other features which are perhaps normally not taught in traditional language programmes. Social interaction can also be in English.
- *Tablets/Smartphones*: The language can be configured to English, thereby requiring the learner to acquire another set of unique vocabulary and other language forms. The S Voice feature in Samsung mobile devices, SIRI in Apple, and equivalents for other brands can allow learners to practice interaction in spoken English on a limited scale for their daily needs.

As for commercial suppliers of MALL and online resources, perhaps it would be advisable to create simulations of 'real-life' apps as part of their mobile-compatible learning management systems that learners can use to complement their own favourites. Automated speech is already a common feature that could be added to these apps, as is voice recognition, which would serve to enhance the learners' listening and speaking skills.

To increase authenticity, all content should be assessed by comparing the language with what would be found in 'real-life' situations. For example, a movie review webpage like www.rogerebert.com presents certain language that is typically associated with describing and judging the quality of movies. Similarly, in their presentation at the 50th IATEFL Conference, Langford and Albair (2016) described how they, as teachers, created a corpus of more than 2 million words based on online restaurant reviews; interestingly enough, as one example, they found the word 'but' being mainly present in three-star reviews and not present at all for one- or five-star entries. Certainly, the power of authentic language for learning is evident, and as much of that language should be introduced as soon as the curriculum calls for it. Over time, artificiality of the language will decrease and authenticity will increase, with progressive cycles of recycling that should reintroduce the theme and genre until an optimal level of authenticity is reached.

International Benchmarks

Another crucial vetting criterion is the correspondence of the content to international standards or benchmarks. There are many, including the Common European Framework of Reference to Languages (CEFR), the American Council on the Teaching of Foreign Languages (ACTFL), World Class Instructional Design & Assessment (WIDA) and TESOL K–12, among others. Rather than define what 'correct English' is or which variety (e.g. British, American, Australian, Singaporean, etc.) to teach and use, they describe the competencies, knowledge, skills and abilities language learners should possess as they move along the proficiency development spectrum over time.

From a practical perspective, perhaps the simplest way to ensure that all online or MALL content is aligned with international standards is by applying learning goals, objectives, outcomes and standards (LGOOS) statements (Mercado, 2015a) during the content development or selection stage. The first three come from the curriculum, and the standards part of the string refers to a proficiency-level descriptor for a skill or language feature being taught that is closest in purpose and meaning to the previous three. Some examples are given in Table 4.1.

In the end, regardless of whether one uses LGOOS statements or not, the language competency, knowledge, skill or ability that is to be enhanced through an online platform or

Table 4.1 Sample LGOOS Statement Strings

Goal	Objective	Outcome	Standard (CEFR *Can Do* Descriptor)
The student will be able to communicate preferences related to food and places.	The student will order food in a restaurant.	The student can order a starter, entrée and a beverage, using *will have* or *would like*.	*A2: Can give a simple description or presentation of people, living or working conditions, daily routines, likes/dislikes, etc., as a short series of simple phrases and sentences linked into a list.*
The student will be able to summarize viewpoints on a social issue.	The student will give a presentation on the topic of her/his choice in relation to family as a social structure.	The student can present information on a complex social issue related to families, using cleft sentences, conditional statements and relevant vocabulary.	*C1 (sustained monologue): Can give clear, detailed descriptions of complex subjects.* *Can give elaborate descriptions and narratives, integrating sub-themes, developing particular points and rounding off with an appropriate conclusion.*

MALL alternative should have a reference to an international standard or benchmark. At the very least, there should be one source to consider, as in the examples above. However, we may want the content to comply with or reflect not just one set of standards or benchmarks, but two or even three. To illustrate, in the examples above it could also be fitting to include technology standards, such as those published by the TESOL International Association. When the content is classified according to proficiency band or level using this vetting process, there can be a stronger claim that the curriculum is highly aligned with international standards and benchmarks, thus enhancing the perception of quality of the content and overall credibility of the programme.

Another pedagogical criterion of importance is the degree of similarity between online or MALL content and what you will find on an international proficiency examination. Nowadays, in a high-stakes, results-driven context for English language teaching and learning, international proficiency examinations are fast becoming a means to validate the quality and credibility of language study programmes, especially in the EFL context. For example, I advocated and eventually instituted the mass implementation of international proficiency examinations at all levels throughout the study programmes for which I was responsible. By having people ranging in age from young children to adult professionals take a variety of international proficiency exams upon their completion of different stages in their respective study programmes, I was able to find a highly credible means of measuring their language development and verify whether it was consistent with programme level goals and objectives. As stated earlier in this chapter, the quality of a study programme is derived from the maximization of learning and the fulfilment of stakeholder expectations, which include how much they believe they have learned compared to what they believe they should have learned over a period of time. When results are positive, then chances are that the learners will be satisfied and continue their studies.

As a growing trend, international proficiency examinations are being used by schools, universities, other educational institutional institutions and ministries of education throughout the world for learner placement and measuring the degree and quality of student learning. Therefore, it may be highly advisable to have a percentage of online or MALL content bear some similarity to what learners will encounter on an international proficiency examination should they be required or opt to take one. It should be noted, however, that by no means am I advocating what is often referred to as 'teaching to the test', which research and experiential, anecdotal data – particularly in general education – have shown to be mostly counterproductive (Volante, 2004; Vaughn, 2015) Popham (2001) makes a distinction between **item teaching**, which can centre an excessive number of hours of instruction on actual or 'look-alike' items that are likely to be found on a standardized test, and **curriculum teaching**, which has teachers concentrate on content knowledge or cognitive skills that are represented on a test. There should be a clear advocacy for the second over the first.

Concurrently, there should both an 'integrated' curriculum and a 'parallel' curriculum that include material whose purpose is mainly to enhance student learning and also familiarize learners with content types, formats and conditions they will encounter on a standardized test should they eventually take one. When vetting content for online platforms and MALL, I would advise having up to 20 per cent related in some form to an international proficiency examination. However, the purpose is not to merely to repeat content, but rather to focus on the skills and knowledge needed to perform well. For example, a common activity on speaking tests is to have learners compare two pictures that are very similar but still have some differences; the language skill is using speaking to communicate the differences. An online or MALL alternative will present two pictures and ask the learner to state or select the differences from a list of options. The presentation of the L2 prompts is very similar to what will appear on an international

ACTIVITY

Before assigning a reading from the Internet or an LMS for home-work, take your students to the multimedia language lab to have them check their comprehension of the words. They should iden-tify the words they fully understand, those they are not sure of and those they are not familiar with at all. Have them calculate the percentage of known words to the total. Is it at least 90 per cent? If not, they may need another reading that is more appropriate.

proficiency examination, but the actual goal is for students to employ grammar and vocabulary to describe the differences. In real life, one may be asked to compare two TVs, two cars, two people or even two approaches, so the learning goal shared by both the test and the platform is sound.

In the end, familiarity with test content types and testing conditions, without relegating quality learning as the main focus, will help students better confront the real test once it is time to take it.

Research and Applied Linguistics

For effective *curricular vetting*, one should not forget the importance of making certain it reflects the findings of rele-vant research studies as well as mainstream pedagogical theory and practice. For example, in reference to vocabulary learning in an ESL/EFL context, it is widely believed that language learners who acquire the 2000 most frequent words in the English language, along with the 570 base words that appear on the *Academic Word List* (AWL), are likely to perform satisfactorily in an exceptionally wide range of spoken conversational situations and understand a similar variety of reading texts (Nation, 2008a). From another perspective, Nation and Waring (1997) go on to establish 95 per cent comprehension of a text as the threshold level in which learners can generally guess the meaning of unknown words on their own. They go on to say that 'the learner needs to know the 3000 or so high frequency words of the language. These are an immediate high priority and there is little sense in focusing on other vocabulary until these are well learned' (p. 11). Taking these insights into account, it would make sense for teachers, curriculum developers and materials designers to assign explicit vocabulary learning a high priority. Teachers may want to resort to vocabulary-building websites, such as www.freerice.com, corpora such as Brigham Young University's Corpus of Contemporary American English (COCA), or student-developed wikis for new words. Online platform designers should consider including features such as digital vocabulary learning logs that would allow learners to build up their vocabulary, with the priority being the most frequent words in English, as suggested by the General Service List (GSL), New General Service List (NGSL), Academic Word List (AWL) or University Word List (UWL), among other well-known compilations of lexical items.

When vetting content for vocabulary learning, using research in support, the teacher or other evaluator of the content has to ask the following questions:

- Is the L2 input presented to maximize the probability that learners will comprehend the new words as a first step so they can recognize and recall them again later (e.g. text, audio, visual, video, etc.)?
- Is the technique or procedure required for learning and practicing the vocabulary consistent with research?
- Will there be an opportunity to recycle the vocabulary later on?
- Is the L2 input associated with an opportunity for learners to produce the language in a communicative situation later on, either autonomously or in class?

Other Criteria

As a final criterion for content evaluation at the programme level, there should be enough quality content to account for the number of instructional hours that are normally associated with the attainment of proficiency levels. If the total content for an LMS does not comply with referential norms, it can be much harder to see discernable progress in the learners' development over time. Plainly stated, the contention that a 100 per cent online programme with a total duration of 300–400 hours will get learners up to a consolidated C1 level of proficiency, as some e-learning providers may claim, may be open to debate. Of course, learning through online and MALL media is not the same as face-to-face instruction, but a certain degree of correspondence should be established nonetheless.

In the post-delivery stage, when content has been accessed and used for learning, there are a variety of ways to determine whether it was useful, relevant or beneficial to learners. A 'red flag' feature would allow learners to identify prompts, exercises, tasks or activities in general that have been characterized by a technical problem or that were not considered particularly useful from the end-user's perspective. The data could be collected systematically so that corrective measures could be taken as soon as possible. Surveys at the end of each learning path or unit could also provide valuable insights on whether learners consider the content helpful. Activity logs and other analytic data could identify the kinds of content that learners use most often and thus consider most engaging or in line with their needs. The system could even suggest content based on previous learner activity, a feature already present when using Netflix to watch movies or Amazon to buy books. In the end, the systematic collection of data from an online platform and its conversion to illustrative statistics on performance or achievement should be a regular feature. With MALL alternatives, the same could be done, taking into account the different formatting requirements, of course.

Conclusion

In this chapter, we have seen the many ways in which content for online and mobile learning alternatives can be vetted for its inclusion in the curriculum. The complexity of the cognitive processes involved, the degree of correspondence between the content and international standards and benchmarks, and the level of authenticity in terms of 'real-world' situations and contexts are but several of the many possible criteria. What is most important is that the content be vetted to ensure quality learning will take place. Only then will results be enhanced and learning satisfaction maximized.

Discussion Questions

1. Why is the provision of L2 input so important for online learning and MALL alternatives? What are some criteria by which L2 input can be assessed?
2. What is a simple way to identify the level of cognitive complexity for a task or activity? Does such a technique apply to lower-level elementary English courses?
3. Is *situational learning* actually achievable from a practical, 'real-world' perspective? Which language skills are the ones that most stand to benefit from it?
4. How familiar are you with international standards? Which framework would you use to vet content for Internet-based reading activities?
5. Is helping learners encounter content that is similar to what they will find on an international proficiency examination good for them or just 'teaching to the test'? What should be the main focus so it is not just the latter?
6. What research do you think is important to consider when vetting online or MALL content? What does research say about grammar learning, for example, and how could that be considered?

Suggested Readings

Beatty, K. (2013) Beyond the Classroom: Mobile Learning the Wider World (Monterey, CA: The International Research Foundation for English Language Education) (accessed http://www.tirfonline.org/wp-content/uploads/2013/12/TIRF_MALL_Papers_Beatty.pdf).
Establishes a link between MALL and *situated learning*, having teachers and students participate as material developers.

Cennamo, K. S., J. D. Ross and P. A. Ertmer (2013) *Technology Integration for Meaningful Classroom Use: A Standards-Based Approach* (Boston: Wadsworth Cengage Learning).
Offers insights on how to effectively integrate technology throughout the curriculum from a standards-based perspective.

Mercado, L. A. (2012) Chapter 7: 'Guarantor of Quality Building & Assurance', in M. A. Christison and F. A. Stoller (eds) *A Handbook for Language Program Administrators*, 2nd edn (Miami, FL: ALTA Vista Books).
Offers an extensive discussion on the quality of language programmes and addresses curricular vetting.

CHAPTER 5

Technology for Speaking and Listening

> *Research has repeatedly demonstrated that teachers do approximately 50 to 80 percent of the talking in classrooms.*
> Bailey, 2003, p. 55

Undoubtedly, becoming a good speaker of English is an aspiration for most English as a second language/English as a foreign language (ESL/EFL) language learners. Of the four main language skills, speaking is the one that is the most needed for face-to-face communication, in person or online, with people from all over the world. It would seem that it is also the most difficult to master because it requires so much from the language user, mostly without previous preparation. Perhaps this is why it is the aspect of language learning that generally receives the most attention from learners, teachers, materials developers and study programmes. Yet, effective speaking cannot take place in isolation as it also depends a great deal on well-developed listening skills and an adequate amount of comprehensible, contextually meaningful L2 input. Therefore, learners should develop their speaking and listening skills together if they are to achieve communicative competence across a wide range of real-life situations (Richards, 2006). With a skilful use of new technologies and e-resources, learners can take their speaking and listening skills to new heights. It is also possible to overcome the excessive teacher-talk time, lack of learner confidence, lack of time to develop comprehension and other challenges long associated with the traditional classroom.

McCarthy (2010) affirms that in order to achieve fluency in conversational interactions 'involving two or more parties, the imperative to create and maintain flow ceases to be the sole responsibility of the single speaker within the single speaking turn and becomes a joint responsibility for all participants' (p. 8). In support, he calls on 'research [that] suggests that ... oral narrative skills are boosted or dampened by the active or inactive behaviour of listeners' (p. 10). Murphy (1991) highlights the importance of listening in interpersonal communication as an 'interactive, interpretive process in which listeners engage in a dynamic construction of meaning. While attending to spoken language, listeners predict topic development, use a series of definable microlistening sub-skills, relate what they hear to their personal stores of prior knowledge and creatively react to what speakers say' (p. 56). In summary, being a good listener is just as important as being a good speaker.

The role of technology in advancing a learner's speaking and listening skills is to facilitate the means for communicative interaction in the classroom or outside of a formal instructional setting. With technology, learners can fine-tune pronunciation, develop a repertoire of speaking or listening strategies, engage in live interaction with people in distant places and self-assess their progress over time, among other potential applications. In addition, teachers can provide feedback to recorded speech samples.

Listening and Speaking Cycle

I would like to postulate a process model that encompasses to a large extent what generally occurs when learners' speaking and listening skills are called upon concurrently at various stages during a typical ESL/EFL classroom or virtual lesson. It could be considered an adaptation of *process instruction* (PI), as described by Van Patten and Cadierno (1993). What I wish to offer in Figure 5.1 is a schematic depiction of the listening-speaking process from the classroom practitioner's perspective, one that perhaps is more amenable to the application of technology in any learning situation:

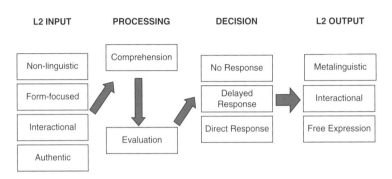

Figure 5.1 'Listening-Speaking Cycle' for the classroom or virtual lesson.

There must first be a purpose or reason before one engages in communication. At the beginning of each listening-speaking cycle, learners may receive input in the L2 that is non-linguistic, form-focused, interactional or authentic. The first kind is something as simple as a picture or symbol about which learners are meant to think and then express themselves, with prior instructions or guiding questions from the teacher. The second is more predominantly teacher initiated and takes the form of explanations regarding grammar, vocabulary, pronunciation, learning strategies or any other form of explicit language training. Interactional input refers to any language that supports activities and tasks that learners must perform or that which is produced by the learners to communicate with each other during such learning events. Authentic content is non-graded and provided by teachers but still serves a pedagogic purpose in class or online; it is also that which is generated by learners in free, uncontrolled situations.

As for the processing stage, the focus here is on what prompts learners to respond. Comprehension is when learners process the information and then evaluate how meaningful it is in relation to their needs, expectations and preferences. They also evaluate whether they are in a position to speak in response. They must decide whether: (i) not to respond because they have not understood enough or are simply not engaged; (ii) to wait until others respond first, building up their courage and confidence in the process; or (iii) to respond immediately because the content has their interest and they feel they are prepared enough.

When the learner has decided to respond, the L2 output can take various forms. It can be metalinguistic, which would be learner-initiated language that describes or explains the language being taught, reviewed and practised. It can be interactional, taking place as learners carry out communicative activities and tasks. There is also free expression, which refers to another form of L2 output from learners that is not produced within the framework of a timed, teacher-guided activity or task, but rather at any other time learners are invited to express themselves freely. Examples include when learners engage in a spontaneous, open-ended classroom discussion or when they produce classroom language to interact as needs arise outside of controlled activities. All of these output types can also be channelled through e-media and can be synchronous or asynchronous in nature.

Most of the time, learners will participate in the listening-speaking cycle depicted above as they carry out purposeful and effective oral communication in pedagogical situations. Yet the key is that they be engaged and attentive to opportunity. In their review of the research and literature on the maximization of learner engagement, Taylor and Parsons (2011) found that instruction should foster interaction, exploration, relevancy of content and the use of multimedia and technology, among other factors. Moreover, one study on the use of technology to increase learner engagement found that 'cell phones, iPhones™ and … and other mobile devices … have been shown to increase [learner] engagement by as much as 78%' (p. 14). This implies that for the

ACTIVITY

For your next lesson in class or online, identify the students who participate voluntarily and who wish to be first. What are their characteristics as learners? What about those who usually participate last or who do not participate at all? Conduct a survey and ask your students why they chose to participate or not. For the next lesson, take their feedback into consideration and see if you can increase participation.

L2 input stage, technology is likely to make the delivery of content more effective, motivating and time efficient, as well as foster social interaction. Here are some practical ideas to keep in mind when enacting the listening-speaking cycle with the support of technology and within the QLL Dynamics framework:

- Practical examples:
  - Classroom:
    - *Interactional/Free expression*: Students are asked to go to the Pinterest website, either on their mobile device or on a computer in the multimedia learning lab. The site offers personalized collections of pictures. Students must find a picture they like. Then they work with a partner to describe the picture and express their feelings about it, practising question making in the process. Afterwards, they report on their partners' feelings about the picture to the class. Finally, the teacher shows certain pictures on the screen, from among those students have proposed, in order to hold a class discussion.
    - *Metalinguistic*: The teacher presents a grammar point in class using PowerPoint Office Mix, with inserted videos and animated grammar explanations. Students then go to the multimedia lab to access the British National Corpus (BNC), Brigham Young University's Corpus of Contemporary American English (COCA), or other source of authentic language, to find real-life examples of how the new grammar is used. Then different

groups of students offer their explanations and examples of the grammar to the rest of the class.

- *Interactional*: The teacher presents a slide show about a couple who has had problems with their relationship. The audio in the background narrates a story, and the questions at the end prompt the students to find a solution to the problem. As the marriage counsellors and one or both members of the couple, they will role play the situation in groups of threes, or they will explain to the audience what to do in such situations.

○ Home:
- *Free expression*: Students can use the *Instaquote* or *Mematic* apps to add text to pictures and create memes or other types of thought-provoking images. They bring the pictures to class, either in print form, a USB or on their mobile device and share them with their classmates for discussion and question-making practice. Another idea is to create a virtual art gallery in groups, with each group presenting their art gallery through a wiki or blog, which can be viewed in a multimedia lab or on a mobile device. Their classmates ask questions about the pictures or share their impressions as if they were critiquing them.
- *Metalinguistic/interactional/free expression*: Teachers can interact with their students through Skype, Google Hangouts™, or Moodle (integrated with WizIQ™ or BigBlueButton™ to allow video conferencing) when the course is 100 per cent online. What kind of L2 output learners reproduce/produce will depend on the language prompts they receive and the tasks or activities they are expected to perform.
- *Free expression/interactional*: The teacher provides students with instructions on how to find TV commercials on YouTube or Vimeo in relation to the lesson's theme or topic. Students watch a particular commercial. They e-mail the link to the commercial to the teacher. In class the next day, students describe the commercials and what they liked most about them. Then the teacher randomly plays three to five of the commercials students sent by e-mail. Students prepare an oral survey and interview each other in class to find out which one was the most popular.

Antonio Galimberti, a teacher in Lima, Peru, offers another example of an activity that promotes interactional speech. It is called *0.5 – Normal – 0.5*, and the goal is to help students develop fluency through repetition and using prompts. Designed with an A1–A2 CEFR level in mind, the teacher first plays the video and models the interaction: one person reads the questions (that appear in the video), and the other answers the questions (with short answers based on the pictures in the video). The steps are as follows:

1. Students are asked to work in pairs. Before playing the video, the teacher changes the speed at which the video will be played, using one of the YouTube set-up tools from Normal to 0.5 so that students can have enough time to get familiar with the activity.
2. Students are asked to change partners. In pairs, they should do the same activity but at Normal speed.
3. Students should ask a question that involves personalization. Play the video at 0.5.
4. This time the video is not played. The teacher just displays the pictures in the video so that students can come up with their own questions.

The following link provides the illustration: https://www.youtube.com/watch?v=N9APLW0va48.

L2 Output-Based Models and Practice

In second-language acquisition theory and research, much is also said about the importance of L2 output and its contribution to the language learning process. Swain (2000) has postulated the *comprehensible output hypothesis*, which asserts that when learners notice a lack of comprehensibility in their output after interacting with others, they rephrase or restructure it to make themselves better understood, reflecting on and learning from it in the process. This is very similar to the concept of *negotiation of meaning.* In her view, output can 'push learners to process language more deeply – with more mental effort – than does input' (p. 99). As for her concept of 'collaborative output' in the L2, this has learners think about and discuss language features as they carry out a communicative task or activity. She points out that it is 'where language use and language learning can co-occur' (p. 97). In support, she cites various studies in which learners who employed metacognitive strategies silently and metacognitive strategies with external verbalization outperformed those who did not do either. This provides a strong indication that 'collaborative output' is likely to help learners develop strategic learning competencies in addition to accuracy in linguistic form during language production. Krashen (1998) has questioned the validity of output hypotheses in general, arguing that learner output is mostly rare and that negotiation of meaning – a feature of L2 output that is advocated by Swain, Long (1996) and others – is even more so. However, as a first-hand witness to the effectiveness of output-oriented pedagogical models, such as the QLL Dynamics framework I have proposed in this volume, I would have to say that perhaps this viewpoint is debatable. In addition to motivational factors that are inherent to the learner, whether or not output takes place as well as the amount and types that can be expected depend largely on the effectiveness of instruction. Much will depend on how good the teacher is at promoting increased Student Talk Time (STT). The QLL Dynamics framework can contribute enormously to such an effort.

Applying These Principles and Concepts in a Twenty-first-century Learning Environment

To enact the collaborative L2 output as described by Swain (2000), there should be a record of the learners' thought processes and constructive dialogues as they work together in pairs or groups. From an instructional perspective, the practice does not have to be done all of the time. Instead, teachers should identify opportunities during the lesson planning process for the kind of collaborative, form-focused dialogue Swain (2000) advocates, and adapt communicative activities and tasks accordingly. Here are some ideas that use technology:

- IWB: The initial prompt can be provided by the teacher. For example, students could work with a sample dialogue and personalize it so that it reflects their own identities and preferences. In groups, one student can be the record keeper and take notes of all of the changes to the original sample until a final version is created. Then, students can act out their new dialogues with the inclusion of the target grammar and vocabulary. At any time during the process, a simple cell phone or smartphone voice recorder can be used to record the dialogue, which can be shared with the teacher or other students via Messenger, WhatsApp, Skype, or e-mail, among other alternatives. The teacher can then assess the level and degree of collaborative form-focused reflection, particularly in terms of how it relates to the final product.
- Skype conference: Students carry out a communicative task online and in their own free time through Skype, for homework. The dynamic is the same, with each participant contributing to a role play, which will be acted out in class the following day. The collaborative dialogue can be recorded by free apps, such as MP3 Skype recorder or Pamela, and then sent to the teacher for review and possible grading. As with the classroom-based alternative, an important part of the interaction is the collaborative discussion and construction of the target language.

In the classroom, at home or any other place of their choosing, learners can record their metalinguistic language and fine-tune their discourse over time.

ACTIVITY

Identify students with similar backgrounds (e.g. age, proficiency level, achievement, etc.) and put them into two groups. If it is a homogenous class, let one group engage in collaborative output using their L1 and the other while using only the L2. If it is heterogeneous, let one group engage in trained collaborative output while the other receives no instructions to do so. Are the samples different (e.g. length, vocabulary, accuracy, etc.)?

E-Learning, Blended and Flipped Solutions

In terms of practising speaking outside of a classroom setting, technology has come a long way. Of course, there are certain limitations as to how much practice learners can get, as speaking depends so much on personal interaction with real people. Nevertheless, e-learning solutions can serve as highly effective means to help learners fine-tune specific strategies and sub-skills. Today, for example, it is not uncommon for most e-learning platforms to include controlled speaking tasks, which have the learner interact with a computer avatar or animated figure. In such cases, the learner responds to the 'computer partner' either by repeating the scripted responses that appear on the screen or by offering an open-ended response, both of which can be recorded, reviewed and repeated. This is as if students were at home practising a variation of the *Read, Look Up, and Say* technique, which is grounded in the notion of 'deliberate practice.' The goal of 'deliberate practice' is to allow learners to keep 'the information in [their] short-term memory long enough for it to move to long-term memory. Once it is in long-term memory, it can be built upon to create more and more complex associations' (Brabeck, Jeffry and Fry, 2015, *Human Memory* section, p. 3). Needless to say, this can help learners later on with their live performances and interactions in the classroom or – most importantly – 'real-life' situations.

Other speaking practice exercises are more realistic because they allow learners to choose from more than one possible response to each of the avatar's lines. Consequently, the practice dialogues can vary significantly with each attempt. Some e-learning platforms allow for synchronous video conferences between the teacher and one or more students, in which case the participants get to carry out speaking activities and tasks live, as if they were in the classroom. Ultimately, what is most important for learners engaged in blended learning programmes with these features is that they eventually have an opportunity to prove that they have learned on their own by performing successfully once they return to the classroom.

In a flipped learning environment, making comprehensible L2 input available by way of language presentations and the introduction of new vocabulary is often the norm. However, it is also important to prepare learners for their expected performances in class by having them do some preliminary speaking practice on their own through e-learning speaking and listening exercises. Practising in advance will build up the learners' confidence as they prepare to engage in more challenging spoken language practice, having additional time to think about and prepare for what will be covered in class the next day (Mercado, 2012a). This will help all students, but particularly the weaker and shy ones, thus reducing their reliance on what Scrivener (2005) would call 'up-in-the-head knowledge' for spontaneous language production. However, to achieve optimal results, there must be a direct correlation between the content in the classroom study materials and that which is on the e-learning platform. Ideally, these should be interchangeable in order to make the autonomous learning environment as amenable to flipped learning as possible.

In Chapter 4, we discussed the use of *Let's Speak* material in blended or fully online learning programmes as a means of providing additional support to prepare students for their video conference sessions with their virtual tutors. As an example of how they can help students speak better, Figure 5.2 shows two transcripts of dialogues that were carried out as part

ACTIVITY

Describe to your students what the speaking task will be the next day, and then refer them to content you have created for them to review at home and practise. Does it help them participate more and produce better language the next day? How can you tell?

Task A	Task B
M: ¿Qué le pregunto? ¿Quién es?	T: Good evening, madam. May I help you?
T: But in English …	M: Good evening. Yes. Yes, sir.
M: What's … What's her … ¿Qué le digo? ¿Cómo le pregunto? ¿Quién es ella?	T: Would you like anything to drink?
	M: I'd like a Coke.
	T: A coke?
T: … name.	M: Yes.
M: What is her name?	T: Are you ready to order?
T: Her name is Emma Watson.	M: Yes. I'd like … Cómo se dice el pan? Por
M: What's her …?	ejemplo, el pan al ajo.
T: Where …	T: Bread, garlic bread.
M: Where is country?	M: I'd like garlic bread.
	T: And what would you like for a main course?
T: No. 'Where is she from?' Repeat, please.	M: I'd like fettuccini.
M: Where is she from?	T: And what would you like for dessert?
T: She's from the United Kingdom. Continue.	M: I'd like … ¿cómo digo? ¿Ice cream? I'd like ice cream.
M: … What's age? What's old?	T: Good. Was everything alright? Did you enjoy the meal?
T: No … How …	M: Yes! Thank you!
M: How old are she?	
T: 'Are she?' Or 'Is she?'	Role reversal:
M: Is she.	
T: Repeat the question, please.	M: Good evening, sir.
M: How old is she?	T: Good evening, madam.
T: She's 25 years old. Okay. Continue.	M: May I help you?
	T: Yes. I'd like to eat.
M: … ¿Cómo le digo?	M: Would you like anything to drink?
T: Is she married or single?	T: Yes, please. A glass of chicha.
M: She is married or single?	M: Are you ready to order?
T: No. It's a question.	T: Yes, please. I want a hamburger with potato chips,
M: ¿Entonces qué le digo? Is she?	and with mayonnaise and ketchup and mustard.
T: Is she married or single?	M: Wow! What would you like for a main course?
M: Is she married or single?	T: The hamburger is the main course.
T: She is single. Continue with the occupation.	M: What would you like for dessert?
	T: I'd like a vanilla ice cream.
	M: Was everything alright?
	T: Yes, everything was perfect. Thank you. It was delicious.

Figure 5.2 Two transcripts of dialogues between a teacher and a student during a video conference.

of an academic study. The study was entrusted to Ricardo Valle, the e-learning manager on my team. In the first scenario, Mirtha, a true novice student just beginning her first course, had not prepared in advance. For the second scenario, she prepared at least two days in advance with the *Let's Speak* content, which was tailor-made for the course:

We can clearly see that the student improves notably with support, producing twice as much language in half the amount of time. The language is also more accurate with less of a tendency to use the L1.

Differentiated Instruction

In the areas of content and language integrated learning (CLIL), content-based learning (CBL) and others in which content and instruction are highly differentiated (e.g. English for specific purposes [ESP], English for academic purposes [EAP], English for professional purposes [EPP]), there is also a role through technology. Many of the principles for successful learning in these areas apply much as they do in general education and second-language acquisition. Among the elements needed to improve the chances of success for language learners in content-centred courses, Mehisto, Marsh and Frigols (2008) cite the following, with additions I have included to make them more technology-based:

- *Create a safe environment for learning*: In the classroom and multimedia language lab, learners can engage with the learning process with technological tools and resources with which they are thoroughly familiar and comfortable, thus reducing anxiety and the hesitance to participate. Technology allows them to practise as many times as they want, self-assess, receive feedback and focus on those areas that are of most interest to them, all of which can help them feel safe and build up their confidence.
- *Consistently use the L2*: With the right input (e.g. content, prompts and instructions) and well-designed tasks and activities, learners

will be keen on using the L2 most or all of the time. At home or on their mobile devices, learners can get all of the L2 input and practice they need, which compensates for the absence of the language in real-life situations and contexts, especially in EFL settings.

- *Use an appropriate level of language*: Flipped classrooms often offer rich content, which can be made more comprehensible when the teacher has recorded the video lesson or when it has already been created by a publisher or e-learning provider.
- *Create opportunities for practice through repetition*: LMSs and other technology-based learning media promote practice through repetition. Learners can self-assess the degree to which their utterances match the language models and repeat exercises as often as needed.
- *Provide a variety of language models*: Course book audios, Internet-based podcasts, YouTube videos and other sources can provide the variety of language models that are needed to train the ear for different accents and speaking speeds.
- *Recognize student effort and success*: When students work on their own using the institutional LMS, the Internet or other technology, they should receive recognition for their efforts. Technology-based learning resources allow the kind of feedback learners expect, whether it is automated or comes from the teacher.

In line with these points, here is an example of a flipped learning lesson for CLIL, titled *'Spartacus: The Gladiator Who Made History'*, that adheres to the QLL Dynamics framework:

1. The teacher informs students that they must learn as much as possible about Spartacus, the historical figure from ancient Roman times. The teacher suggests the following webpage as a starting point:http://www.bbc.co.uk/history/historic_figures/spartacus.shtml. By way of the institutional Intranet, the teacher adds a brief recorded lecture of four minutes using PowerPoint Mix. Links to segments of the Spartacus series and documentaries on YouTube as well as information from other websites are also provided in order to enrich the students' mental imagery and understanding of the topic.

2. Students are told in advance of what the activities in class will be the following day and throughout the rest of the week.
3. Students perform in class after they have worked on their own:
   a. Day 1: Class discussion – Teacher and students discuss what they found and give general impressions of Spartacus as the man who led a rebellion against Rome.
   b. Day 2: Role play – Each group designates three students to act out a short segment from their favourite scene from the *Spartacus* series or something described in the documentaries. Then they must explain the situation and how it relates to the historical context. Each group shows video or images from the series or documentaries on the projection screen or monitor after they have performed.
   c. Day 3: Group presentation – Students complete graphic organizers that describe Spartacus and details from what they were able to find. They summarize the information for their group on the class blog. An app like *MindMash* can also be used to facilitate the drawing of the graphic organizers.
   d. Days 4 and 5: Wiki development – A class wiki is created on *Spartacus* with the whole classes' contributions after the teacher has organized the information into different segments. Work is done in the multimedia language lab and at home. The final version is reviewed and discussed in the multimedia language lab on the last day.

Going beyond more 'conventional' content on the Internet, a truly unique opportunity for speaking practice is *Second Life*. It offers an excellent opportunity through its *nearby* (spatial) *chat*, *individual chat* or *group chat* functions. There are technical requirements and not all of the environments in the virtual world are voice enabled. However, when they are, it is possible to hear other people's voices in the background, have a private one-to-one conversation or talk within a group. If a task is designed well enough, students can be assigned to enter the *Second Life* world and converse with other 'inhabitants', using English as the main medium of communication. With the consent of the other participants, the chats can even be recorded, although apps like *Audacity* for Windows or *Garage Band* for iOS

ACTIVITY

Explore Second Life and create a homework assignment or course project that requires your students to interact with others in the virtual world and later report on what they saw, whom they met, what they liked and so on.

may have to be used concurrently and with some prior configuration. These recorded chats can be submitted for review or grading purposes. They can also be shared with the class and used for discussion as well as form- and meaning-focused activities. In the near future, forward-thinking institutions and e-learning providers can create virtual 'places' of their own in which students can interact with teachers, each playing their roles and using English in a variety of virtual settings and situations (e.g. office, school, street, presentations, ordering food, etc.).

Focus on Listening

As stated earlier, listening comprehension is a vital skill that is required for effective spoken communication because the person not actually speaking during a particular turn in a conversation must listen carefully in order to maintain its flow. As McCarthy (2006) points out, speakers should 'contribute to each others' fluency … scaffold each other's performance and make the whole conversation flow. There is a confluence in the talk, like two rivers flowing inseparable together' (p. 4). Such an accomplishment can only be made possible by an active listener's participation. However, becoming a good listener in a second language is no easy task, and developing a strong syllabus that cultivates good listening skills is perhaps less so.

According to Rost (2015), research sustains that listeners who perform better and demonstrate continuous progress are those who learn and apply effective strategies and critical thinking skills. Moreover, he argues that the 'integration of learning strategies helps students listen more efficiently, and become more autonomous learners who can acquire language on their own... . [The] use of explicit listening strategies can enable students to handle tasks that may be more difficult than their current processing might allow' (pp. 207–208). Another point I would consider important is that the amount and kind of L2 input should be abundant, varied (multiple genre) and aligned to empirically based benchmarks, such as the CEFR. Thirdly, the diversity in the alternatives for listening practice should be consistent with the learner's needs and preferences.

With these important considerations in mind, the path becomes clearer to effective listening instruction. When focusing specifically on listening as the predominant skill to teach, it is perhaps best to keep things simple. Structuring in-class and online lessons so that they provide opportunities for pre-listening, listening, and post-listening tasks may be highly effective, especially if they demand learners to apply metacognitive strategies in the process (NCLRC, 2004). Here are some websites, apps and instructional ideas that can cater to these important aspects of listening skill development:

- *YouTube* or Vimeo videos: Teachers can work with any video after it has been carefully chosen, and assign it for viewing outside of class. Their students can follow a link sent to them by e-mail so they can take a fun quiz to check their listening comprehension.
- Website: Learners can practise their English listening skills by going to a website like the British Council's LearnEnglish Teens, which has a range of audio samples according to CEFR proficiency bands and communicative functions as well as transcripts, picture prompts, test-like question formats, automatic feedback, and downloads. Randall Davis's ESL Cyber Listening Lab offers a wide variety of listening texts and exercises that range in level, topic, type, and length. TED Talks is great for high-intermediate and advanced-level learners as it offers presentations that are given live in front of large audiences on a great variety of topics.

- Mobile Apps: English Listening provides a collection of listening texts of varying complexity and according to topic. The tests on English Listening have question items and listening texts that resemble those that might be found on an international proficiency examination. Podcast Addict allows teachers and learners alike to subscribe to podcasts of almost unlimited genre, personalize the collection, and listen to them on their tablets or smartphones whenever they wish or play them back in the classroom for listening-speaking practice.

Music can also contribute to second-language acquisition, specifically aiding the development of speaking and listening skills. In his review of the literature and research, Engh (2013) contends that this belief is strongly supported by a variety of generally accepted hypotheses, theories and principles, such as integrative motivational theory and the *affective filter* hypothesis. He also refers to the research that highlights important benefits, such as the development of listening comprehension and an improved ability to recall discrete lexical items as well as longer phrases and formulaic expressions. Examples of helpful websites and apps include:

- Lyricstraining.com: Students must complete the lyrics as they listen to a wide selection of songs in different varieties of English. The number of words to complete depends on the level: beginner, intermediate, advanced and expert (all the words). There is a score, time per entry and bonus points (gamification).
- *Learn English with Music*: This is an app with preloaded songs with lyrics that can be translated instantly as students listen to the music. Songs can also be streamed from other sources, along with the respective lyrics. The student's native language can be chosen from a wide variety of options.

In this chapter's section on differentiated instruction, providing a variety of language models was cited as a prerequisite to successful learning. For listening practice, it may be a good idea for teachers to go beyond the variety already offered by

ACTIVITY

Have students practice a song, using either one of the alternatives above, on their own. Then use YouTube to do a karaoke exercise in class. Divide the class into groups, and assign segments of the song to each one. Then have the groups come up front to explain the meaning of at least five new words they have learned, with examples of sentences on how these words can be used.

publishers' course book series and purposefully work with different varieties of English in order to better train the learners' listening comprehension skills. At Euroidiomas in Lima, Peru, for example, the language programme goes from using an American English course book series at the basic and intermediate levels to a strictly British English focus at the advanced level. The goal of the study programme is to get students up to a level of proficiency that will allow them to pass the Cambridge First examination. At the institution, it is believed that using an American English series for the basic and intermediate levels should not keep our students from doing well on any lower-level proficiency examination that may be associated mostly with the British English variety. However, at higher levels, focusing on a specific variety of English in the classroom and in online learning environments can make a difference, most especially for the listening comprehension section. In the case of Euroidiomas, as students get closer to taking the Cambridge First certificate, they are exposed to an ever greater amount of input in British English. Here is an example of a technique for practising listening comprehension for both varieties:

- Play the audio once in American English, and have students do the task. Play the audio a second time, and have them do a different task.

- After playing the American English version of the audio twice, have the students do a third task with the British English version of the same text or content.
- At higher levels, switch the focus so that the first two times are played in British English and the third time is played in American English.

Certainly, if the exit examination were more associated with American English, the roles would be reversed: British English being the greater focus at the lower levels and American English for the high-intermediate and advanced learners. This works best with course book series that have both an American English and a British English version, allowing teachers to work with 'mirrored' audio tracks. In such cases, the audio scripts are essentially the same, just played with different accent varieties. Even when the scripts are not the same, teachers can work with audio samples with different content as long as the language level is roughly the same. Teachers and institutions can also create their own listening tracks with different varieties of English (e.g. Indian, New Zealander, British, etc.) by using text-to-speech software and apps that let you choose the accent variety in which the audio is to be played. Of course, all course series include a significant number of audio texts in international English, which should also be played and worked with in much the same fashion as I have described above, depending on the focus of the lesson, course or language programme. Technology makes it very easy to create and use such resources.

Conclusion

This chapter integrated speaking and listening as essential skills for successful oral communication. Although technology still cannot fully simulate conversational situations between two or more real people, there are many aspects of oral communication with which it can be of great assistance.

Most notably, it can save much needed time by providing the means for individual practice that can serve to build up learner confidence and the prerequisite knowledge and skills needed to support the higher-order thinking tasks that take place in the classroom. As for listening, technology can stream an endless amount of L2 input, and with the proper strategy training and careful content selection, much of it can be understood, processed and integrated as part of the learners' interlanguage. The next chapter discusses reading and writing, the other two essential language skills, using the same approach.

Discussion Questions

1. What kind of L2 input is most advised for speaking and listening practice? What kind of input would you provide your students in preparation for a fluency activity in class the next day?
2. If it were not possible for students to meet in a classroom, how could they still engage in live speaking practice with each other from their homes? What kind of task would you have them do?
3. What is a specific listening skill that is often required on international proficiency examinations? How could you prepare your students for it?
4. What is the most successful YouTube, TED Talks or other video lesson you have used? Why was it so successful?
5. What do you know about *Second Life*? What are some challenges associated with its use to promote listening-speaking practice, and how could you and your students overcome them?
6. How would you go about grading content for listening and then making it available on the Internet?

Suggested Readings

McCarthy, M. and R. Carter (2014) *Language as Discourse: Perspectives for Language Teaching* (New York: Routledge).

Highlights the features of discourse and offers insights on how they can be accounted for in teaching, not only in the traditional classroom but also in virtual environments.

Rost, M. (2015) *Teaching and Researching Listening – Applied Linguistics in Action*, 3rd edn (New York: Routledge).
Offers the most recent insights on SLA research regarding listening instruction, with lessons and insights that can sustain technology-based learning processes.

Rost, M. and J. J. Wilson (2013) *Active Listening: Research and Resources in Language Teaching.* (New York: Routledge).
Expands on the research and ties it to a plethora of practical activities.

6 Technology for Reading and Writing

The relationship between reading and writing is a bit like that of the chicken and egg. Which came first is not as important as the fact that without one the other cannot exist... . Basically put: reading affects writing and writing affects reading.

K–12 Reader, 2015

Among the essential language skills, the practice of reading is perhaps the one through which L2 input can best be processed systematically at the learner's choosing and pace. In terms of its importance, Grabe (2009) contends that citizens in modern societies must be good readers in order to succeed and that '[t]he advent of the computer and the Internet does nothing to change this fact. If anything, electronic communication only increases the need for effective reading skills and strategies as we try to cope with the large quantities of information made available to us' (p. 5). As for writing, nowadays people engage in e-mailing, instant text messaging and posting on social media as activities that are second nature to them, and may find less of a need to write more extensively or formally as in the past. Thus, there is a growing concern as to whether technology is also having a negative impact on the development of general writing skills. According to Lenhart et al. (2008), there are many who feel 'that the quality of writing ... is being degraded by ... electronic communication, with its carefree spelling, lax punctuation and grammar, and its acronym shortcuts. Others wonder [however] if this return to text-driven communication is instead inspiring new appreciation for writing' (p. 2). In both cases, I believe we need not be overly worried. Technology can actually do much to facilitate successful reading and writing, which leads us to the following questions:

- How can technology facilitate the delivery of content for reading purposes in ways that will keep learners highly motivated?
- How can reading in and out of the classroom be integrated through technology?
- Which types of writing should be taught in a technological age? What role does genre play?
- Can social media be used to promote writing skills despite academia's perception that they do the opposite?

As Anderson (2008) points out, reading is essential because it facilitates access to an enormous amount of information in the world. In the twenty-first-century, access to most of that information would not be ipossible without technology. In a traditional face-to-face classroom, for example, teachers generally work with readings in the course book and any additional texts they may find on their own. However, because covering the text according to 'schedule' generally represents an enormous challenge for teachers, there may not be enough time for students to go beyond these initial readings and corresponding comprehension questions. As a result, they may not have the opportunity to practise a variety of strategies that could help them further improve their levels of comprehension, fluency and overall strategic competence in reading. Another potential problem is that the printed readings themselves may not be as engaging as using alternate, technologically supported texts, especially when a sense of choice is lacking. A third limitation is that a traditional approach does not necessarily work towards the attainment of international standards and benchmarks, so the lack of clear goals and performance targets may make the reading of L2 content ineffective and cause learner amotivation to set in. Lastly, standard syllabi often do not promote **extensive reading** as a natural extension of successful **intensive reading**, potentially forfeiting many of the enormous benefits the first has to offer language learners.

Intensive-Extensive Reading

For a reading programme to be successful, there must first be a high degree of motivation to read on the part of learners. Much has been discussed in previous chapters regarding motivation for language learning, but motivation for reading can be a topic of its own. Apparently, there is yet much to be done in order to shed more light on the relationship between learner motivation and certain aspects of reading. According to Grabe (2009), this calls for teachers and other educational stakeholders to further explore the 'relationships between motivation traits and reading measures: reading amount, reading enjoyment, reading strategy use, vocabulary knowledge, and reading comprehension' (p. 190).

Much has actually been said about the effects of extensive, or leisure, learning on learner motivation. Studies have shown it can have a positive impact on learner reading habits and skills, performance on achievement tests and the acquisition of content knowledge. According to Mason and Krashen (1997), a series of studies on extensive reading (ER) in English as a foreign language (EFL) determined that learners who engaged in ER were able to make a significant improvement in their reading performance on standardized achievement tests or outperformed their traditionally taught peers outright. In another study by Hughes-Hassell and Rodge (2007), 584 urban adolescents were asked about their attitudes towards ER, and most of them cited it as a means of relieving boredom, having fun or finding motivation, supporting the view that ER can encourage learners to do more reading and learn more as a result. In a study by Yamashita (2013), 61 undergraduate students studying EFL at a Japanese university demonstrated positive views on ER and a willingness to put it into practice, attitudes which are often considered prerequisites to successful reading in general. Another example is a qualitative study of ER in German as a second language by way of an online reading programme (Arnold, 2008), which showed a variety of affective and linguistic benefits, including the learners' search for more demanding reading materials, conscious decision-making about the use of reading strategies, and regular dictionary use. These and other findings, as well as an endless amount of anecdotal data from teachers, indicate the need to develop a solid reading programme that makes the most out of classroom reading practice and integrates it with ER.

As director, I instituted an intensive-extensive reading programme for tens of thousands of EFL students. In terms of CEFR proficiency bands, the programme covered the A2 through C1 levels and integrated in-class activities with autonomous reading practices. A variety of readings were provided per course level, all of which were graded previously using a specific technique I devised that was based on Flesch-Kincaid measures, number of words and Internet-based resources, such as Compleat Lexical Tutor (Mercado, 2012a; Mercado, 2015b). Readings differed in terms of length and genre, and they were all made available through the institutional Intranet. As a means of ascertaining learner acceptance of the programme, a qualitative survey was conducted with 2945 students (Mercado, 2015b). More than 87 per cent thought that the course book readings were insufficient for enhancing their reading skills, and 79 per cent thought online readings were a good way to continue learning vocabulary. Allowing the students to choose one reading from up to ten different options and then having them perform a follow-up group activity in class, either written or spoken, were perhaps the key elements in determining the success of the programme, which eventually had most of the students engaged in ER. Here are some of the kinds of questions they would answer:

- Who was your favourite character in the story? Why?
- What were the main points of the article or story?
- What is something you didn't like about the story?
- Is there anything that surprised you?
- What are some new words you learned? How were they used in the story?

By using generic questions, students could be grouped together regardless of the reading they chose for the course. They were encouraged to say as much as they could in response to each question, in complete sentences and elaborated ideas. The genre were varied, however, so students could also read articles and other types of text as long as they were included among the options. Here is a small excerpt from a freewriting activity a low-intermediate student completed in response to a *New York Daily News* article:

> A family made a fortune when they won lawsuit against city. They discovered that their dead son's brain was displayed in a jar in a city morgue. They got angry for that. Andre and Trisha ----- had buried their son J--- in 2005 after he was killed when he crashed his car… . The canister was labeled with the boy's name. The -----'s daughter, S-----, came home and told them everybody in school was talking about it, that the medical examiner's office had J----'s brain. Family lawyer Anthony ------- said, 'It's against the law' because the medical examiner had retained the organs after conducting the autopsy on J----'s remains. (*Note:* names intentionally removed)

This selection is particularly interesting because of the very low-frequency vocabulary being used, with words such as *lawsuit, morgue, canister, medical examiner, brain, family lawyer, remains, retained* and even *formaldehyde* at some point. Such words are rarely if ever taught in a typical course book or programme. Yet this student was able to recall the content without referring to the article during the freewriting activity. Other students had similar performances.

ACTIVITY

Find ten reading texts that your students might enjoy, using a survey or similar instrument to determine their likes and preferences. Check to make sure they are at least 95 per cent comprehensible, and have your students read one of them. Design an in-class writing or speaking activity that is based on the reading of their choice. How much of the new language can they use?

Of those surveyed in the study (Mercado, 2015b), 76 per cent opted to read more than the one reading selection that was required for the course, doing so for leisure rather than coursework compliance. In the end, the programme led learners from intensive reading under teacher guidance to extensive reading on their own initiative.

Nowadays, most well-known publishers have online graded readers, with access options that go from free, unrestricted use to accompany their printed materials, to single student licences and one-time yearly institutional fees. Many are also categorized according to general proficiency or, more specifically, the CEFR. It is perhaps the easiest way to obtain appropriate content for a technologically supported intensive-extensive reading programme. Of prime consideration is the need for teachers and other key decision-makers to make certain that students are offered the opportunity to choose the reading they prefer, that various genre are offered, and that word length and proficiency level are appropriate. Although there are no definitive methods for matching reading texts to international standards and benchmarks, such as the CEFR, there are measures to support a more careful selection of available readings. Table 6.1 depicts a referential correspondence table for graded readers that was adapted from an Extensive Reading Foundation (n.d.) scale and applies to any graded reader regardless of the publisher:

Table 6.1 Referential Correspondence of Headwords and Proficiency Levels for Graded Readers

	Referential Proficiency Level				
	Beginner (A1)	Elementary (A2)	Intermediate (B1)	Upper Intermediate (B2)	Advanced (C1 – C1+)
Headwords	1–300	301–800	801–1500	1501–2400	2401–4500

The CEFR can guide teachers in choosing appropriate texts as it can learners if they are adequately trained. Teachers and learners can identify keywords in the CEFR descriptors in order to search for appropriate texts. To illustrate, the B1 descriptor for 'reading correspondence', a sub-type of reading comprehension according to the CEFR states the following: 'Can understand the description of events, feelings, and wishes in personal letters well enough to correspond regularly with a pen friend' (Council of Europe, 2001, p. 69). The key words in this case are 'personal letters', for which an Internet search can be used to find an endless variety of samples.

In Figure 6.1, we see a sequence for finding reading texts and creating a library for instructional or personal use that can help learners consolidate their reading skills in accordance with their current level of proficiency development, or **interproficiency** (e.g. beginning, weak, strong A2) as I would call it, adapting the term from Selinker's interlanguage (1972) concept.

Tasks and question types should account for the level of cognition and language skill competence that is described in the benchmark or standard. As an example, the A1 descriptor for the CEFR sub-skill of 'reading for information and argument' is stated as follows: 'Can get the idea of the content from simpler informational material and short simple descriptions, especially if there is visual support.' Examples of such text types can be

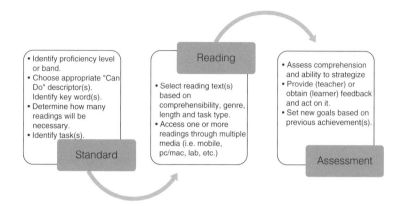

Figure 6.1 Process for selecting readings that correspond to international standards and benchmarks.

found on many websites, such as https://www.londonpass.com, which includes a list of attractions people can visit for free by using their London Pass. Questions like 'Do you have to pay for your favourite attraction?', 'How many days can you use your London Pass?' or 'How much does the London Pass cost?' are in line with the corresponding CEFR descriptor. A similar task could be based on the reservation process at www.brooklyndiner.com, a well-known diner in Brooklyn, New York, or information about Archbishop Molloy High School at http://www.molloyhs.org, an outstanding Catholic high school in Queens, New York. Although these are authentic sites with abundant information, learners

ACTIVITY

Have your class create a library of readings using a class blog, with each student submitting one text he or she would like to share. The readings should reflect different topics and genre. Which ones are the most popular? How many students read more than one?

need only search for specific information whose comprehensibility and ease of localization can be determined by the questions or task themselves, relieving the learners of the need to understand more than what they are prepared for.

Reading Strategy Training

Not only are abundant intensive and extensive reading opportunities important for learners, but also their ability to learn and master reading strategies. They should be trained and asked to practice until they have developed a repertoire that can best suit their needs according to reading genre and length of text. According to Grabe and Stoller (2002), 'Expert readers are able to use a variety of strategies flexibly and in conjunction with one another' (p. 208). Unfortunately, it would seem that most course books do not integrate explicit reading strategy training with their reading activities, and neither do providers of e-learning platforms. Typically, most reading activities require students to skim or scan and then answer a series of general comprehension questions. I asked a publisher to modify the content of the course series we were going to use so that it included explicit training in reading strategies for students. With this modification to the beginning and intermediate-level course books, the strategies would become much more diverse, to include many which Grabe and Stoller (p. 209) consider as vital to developing learner prowess in strategic reading, such as these:

- Identifying a purpose for reading
- Predicting
- Asking questions to yourself
- Summarizing
- Analysing and talking about text structure
- Looking up words in the dictionary
- Connecting one part of the text to the other.

With another experience, when I was asked to design the structure and content map for a young adult/adult online course in English for the Internet customers of a large telecommunications company, the same logic was applied. However, rather than explicitly cite the reading strategy, as was the case for the course book series in the previous example, the questions were designed in a way that required the learner to focus on the meaning but at the same time implicitly use a particular strategy in order to arrive at the right answer. In a way, it was applying Ellis's (2001) Planned Focus-on-Form concept to reading strategy instruction and training. Here is an example of a question:

> What do you think will happen next?
> a. The man will quit his job and change careers.
> b. The man will put up a fight and stay at his place of work.
> c. The man will apologize to his boss and ask her for a second chance.

Of course, the picture prompt and supporting text are supposed to get the learner to think about the logical next step. Whether the answer is correct is not a major concern at this point. What matters most is the process of analysing the information in an attempt to arrive at a prediction of what comes next in the story. The following question at the end will help the learner confirm the right choice or understand why the original selection she or he made was incorrect:

> What made it impossible for the man to put up a fight or ask for a second chance?
> a. The evidence was not in his favour.
> b. The decision had already been made to 'let him go' with his respective compensation.
> c. He was tired and no longer happy with his job.

Certain LMSs allow teachers to change the questions for the online readings in their platforms. Teachers only need to incorporate questions that will get their students to think strategically.

In other cases, texts can be chosen from outside sources and embedded in a content management or open source platform, such as Moodle, Blackboard or Chamilo, after which comprehension and strategy questions can be tailor-made for every learning goal, objective, outcome and standard or LGOOS (Mercado, 2015a) statement. Depending on the age group, there are also websites and apps that can help learners of all ages develop their ability to apply different reading strategies. Here are some examples:

- *Into the Entry* (reading.ecb.org): This website, for younger learners in elementary and middle school, is primarily meant to be used with native speakers but can be adapted for ESL/EFL students. It features explanations of each strategy and videos on how to do the corresponding activities, and provides the opportunity to choose specific strategies and content for practice. It also offers automatic feedback and even a paintbrush for cases involving visualization practice. The website provides learners with hints and allows them the chance to save their work by registering as users.
- *Reading is Fun* (LITE): This app is meant for learners who are native speakers in grades 1–5, but the content is challenging enough for older students. Some of the questions are simple comprehension questions, whereas others require the learner to engage in higher-order thinking and strategies, such as inferencing.
- *IELTS Reading*: This app is designed to prepare learners for the reading section of the IELTS examination. It is appropriate for learners with different levels of proficiency. In addition to checking for comprehension, learners are expected to apply different strategies such as visualizing, inferring and others, to arrive at the right answers.

Reading Fluency

Reading fluency is another measure by which the success of readers in a second language is often determined. Since the 1980s, research has been pointing to automaticity in information processing and an awareness of prosodic features of oral reading and speech (e.g. rhythm, pacing, intonation, etc.) as key factors in reading fluency development (Samuels, 2012). Mainstream instructional practices now include repeated reading, assisted reading and oral reading for fluency. Anderson (2008) defines reading fluency as 'reading at an appropriate rate with adequate comprehension' (p. 66) and considers at least 200 words per minute at 70 per cent comprehension as an adequate goal for intermediate- and advanced-level readers.

In addition to the repeated reading technique and its variants, simply reading more content, freely and extensively, has also been found to contribute to fluency development in numerous studies (Iwahori, 2008; Krashen, 2001; Taguchi, Takayasu-Maass and Gorsuch, 2004). According to the Extensive Reading Foundation (2011), extensive reading is associated with 98 per cent comprehension or above and fast, fluent and enjoyable reading as opposed to instructional reading, which can range between 90 and 98 per cent comprehension, and 'painful', or frustration level, reading at below 90 per cent. In summary, technologically assisted reading practice aimed at improving fluency should consist of L2 input at or below the learners' current level of proficiency and language development. It should also facilitate repeated reading, assisted reading and extensive reading at the learners' own discretion. Here are several online and mobile-assisted language learning (MALL) alternatives that could prove to be very helpful:

- *Fluency Tutor* for Google™: It can be used by way of Google Chrome™ and Google Drive™. The free version allows teachers to assign graded readings to their students, which can be sent by e-mail. Work could be done in a language lab or at home. Students listen and read silently to the highlighted text as it is read aloud by the computer. Then they have the opportunity to read it aloud themselves, recording their voices and saving the files to their hard drive or tablet. When they are satisfied with their sample, they can send it to their teacher for review and assessment. Resources include a dictionary, picture dictionary and a translator. The paid version allows teachers to access statistics on performance metrics for their students, individually and as a group. Such metrics include word count per minute, mispronounced words, reading rate, progress, and so on.

- *Readings with audio*: Publishers now offer audio support for their graded readers and readings in their course books. Similar readings or audiobooks can be found on the Internet on websites such as http://www.manythings.org/listen/, http://www.rong-chang.com/reading.htm and www.projectguttenberg.org, which has a general selection of close to 50,000 e-books. The website http://www.autoenglish.org/listenings.htm has a useful tool that grades any text the user can cut and paste. It is rated according to various well-known indices, such as Gunning Fog, Coleman Liau, Flesch Kincaid (Grade Level and Ease), Automated Readability (ARI) and SMOG (simplified measure of gobbledygook).

- *Self-assessment*: Learners can work with any graded reader or reading of their choice that they deem 100 per cent comprehensible. They read it aloud from their tablet or PC while recording their voices. Then they tally how many words they read in a minute for each try until they believe they are reading at a comfortable, natural rate. From the recording, they should try to discern those words which were incorrectly pronounced or omitted altogether, checking with an online dictionary or other source when uncertain themselves. They can then obtain their own ratings for wpm, error per sample, and accuracy. Teachers can provide their students with a self-assessment checklist.

As for community-building practices, learners can build up an e-portfolio of the readings they have worked with and share them with classmates by way of a reading club or forum on a blog, wiki, content management platform, institutional Intranet, or cloud if the means are so provided. These may include images of texts that are more associated with beginner or elementary students, such as office or street signs, instructions, or restaurant menus. They can share their experiences and advice on how to improve one's reading skills and fluency over time.

ACTIVITY

Have your students work on their reading fluency through one of the alternatives described above. Compare their progress with that of another group that is not using technology to work on reading fluency. How do they compare? How can you modify your teaching strategy to help all of your students?

Writing

Writing in a second language is undoubtedly a difficult task for learners and teachers alike because it is often considered to be so labour-intensive and because it demands a higher level of structure and precision than speaking. It demands a stricter adherence to conventions, planning and language accuracy. On the other hand, the writing process allows a person more time to think about how a message is to be conveyed and reformulate the content if necessary. Although learners may consider it somewhat tedious and less engaging than speaking, it is nonetheless an essential skill without which they cannot make true progress in their proficiency development. As for teachers, they can often find the task of reviewing their students' writings and providing feedback as one of the least attractive and most stressful aspects of the work they do. Yet it can be one of the most fulfilling as well, especially when their students make discernable progress over time. However, without proper instruction, feedback and successful closure to the writing process, students' writing skills will remain poor. This can potentially leave them at an enormous disadvantage in a highly technological, fast-paced world where writing is quickly becoming a much more important form of communication than ever before.

When learning to write in a second language, progress is gradual. In this regard, technology can serve as an important resource to support language learners every step of the way as

ACTIVITY

Have your students do writing tasks for different genres they have seen in the course book before. Analyse and judge their performance. Then have your students analyse explicitly at least four or five genre types and identify the main characteristics of each one. Finally, have them do the writing tasks for the different genres again. Do you see any difference?

they move from words to sentences, paragraphs, multiple paragraphs and ultimately extended discourse. In addition to standard writing conventions, other important elements should be considered in ESL/EFL writing instruction and development, such as genre. Stein and Meyer zu Eissen (2006) affirm that '[g]enre identification shall discover groups of texts that share a common form of transmission, purpose, or discourse properties' (p. 449). Genre can serve to enhance the effectiveness of writing instruction by concentrating the attention of learners on the common elements of a particular type of writing text regardless of the actual topic. Johns (2003) elaborates on this point by referring to genre as a heuristic or facilitating aid for writing because students can associate certain discourse features with the writing task at hand. Additionally, she refers to reader expectations and how genre may influence the writer's form, content and register as context is considered during the writing and revision process. With proper training, this could actually provide much needed guidance to learners and may be one of the keys to writing skill development.

Social Media and Freewriting

Among the many written language genres learners encounter in their everyday lives, one cannot fail to mention social media. Facebook, Instagram, Pinterest, Twitter, Tumblr and others offer learners of all ages the opportunity to express themselves freely in a context that promotes creativity, personalization, intrinsic motivation and a sense of recognition, all of which are elements that generally support any successful writing enterprise. Although many believe that expressing oneself through social media may thwart both L1 and L2 writing skills development, there is recent research that may indicate otherwise. Studies issued by the Department of Education and universities in the United Kingdom have found that texting, tweeting, posting and general communication through social media all offer important benefits for learning. They extend engagement with the language outside of a formal instructional setting, enhance social interaction skills, lead to creativity and free expression and are conducive to higher scores on verbal reasoning and other achievement tests (Miller, 2014). Plester, Wood and Bell (2008) conducted two studies with groups of 10- to 11-year-olds and 11- to 12-year-olds who were asked to translate standard English sentences to text messages, and vice versa. Surprisingly enough, those who performed better on the translation exercise and used a greater number of text abbreviations, or 'textisms', and obtained higher overall verbal reasoning, spelling proficiency and writing scores. They conclusionde that 'while further investigation is in order with respect to all aspects of text message literacy and standard school literacy, these early studies have shown no compelling evidence that texting damages standard English in preteens, and considerable evidence that facility with text language is associated with higher achievement in school literacy measures' (p. 143).

Evidently, there is a potential in written communication through social media that is not yet fully tapped. What seems to explain some of the positive attributes of social media communication is the fact that it is generally brief, spontaneous and efficacious in the use of limited resources, such as time. This concurs with the position that writing is a cognitive process that depends, to a significant extent, on the use of working memory or short-term memory as ideas are translated into text, with sentence, paragraph, document or other schemata being called upon progressively upon need (Kellogg, 2008).

Certainly, one could surmise that such schemata would include texting, tweeting, posting and others. Therefore, all are likely to be beneficial in training working memory for written expression. In Figure 6.2, we find some ideas on how to promote writing skills through social media:

With Facebook, teachers can post pictures and ask their students to write in their response. For example, a picture of spaghetti might be posted, followed by questions like: "What do you see in the picture?" and "What ingredients does it have?" Students can also go around their house, neighbourhood or city and take pictures, posting them onto the community website, with questions eliciting their classmates' responses.

With LinkedIn, students can create their own profiles, listing their previous work experience and other important information about who they are and what they have to offer a company. They can post comments and articles as well as respond to others. They can insert their resume or curriculum vitae, videos, PowerPoint presentations, and other media in English. A goal for a course could be to have the greatest number of posts and their respective responses.

With Twitter, teachers can create special accounts for their own classes and have students respond to their tweets. Students can also create their own and have their classmates respond. In addition, they can sign up and follow trending topics of their choice. Then they can send their Tweets to their teacher for review and assessment. They can also post their own if they have enough followers.

With Tumblr, students can create their own blogs, posting anything from pictures to music, videos, and an endless variety of texts. Teachers can identify and follow their students' blogs for feedback, class discussion, sharing with other social media, and graded project-work.

Figure 6.2 Writing tasks using social media.

In addition to writing for social media, freewriting is another form of less structured, more informal writing that can be of significant benefit to language learners according to research. As opposed to other approaches that have been explored in previous research, Galbraith and Torrence (2004) describe what they consider to be the 'full' form of **interactive writing strategy**: (i) freewriting that leads to an 'undifferentiated mass of content' (p. 71); (ii) identification of main ideas in rough writing sample; and (iii) ideas derived from original sample to construct a whole new text with structure, unless the original sample is well formed

ACTIVITY

Create a group page on Facebook or a Twitter account for one of your classes if you don't have one yet. Post pictures and questions, articles, Tweets, and other content to get your students to respond with a certain number of posts per week. Criteria for writing should be explained beforehand. Compare their writing through social media with what they may produce through more traditional tasks. Which content is more original?

and clearly expressed enough that a revision along more traditional lines may be more appropriate. In a study testing four different types of outline and interactive strategies, they asked the participants to write an article in 50 minutes, dedicating half of the time to the initial draft and the other half to reformulation or revision. Due to the findings, they concluded that planned or traditional outline strategies are more likely to lead to more organized, less discursive or idea-laden written texts, whereas interactive strategies, especially those in which the original draft is unavailable for reference, lead to less structured, more discursive writing. In other words, the interactive approach focuses on thought and idea generation from the beginning whereas the outline approach does so more timidly within the constraints that are imposed by the need to comply with text organization and other writing conventions. Consequently, they suggest that from an instructional perspective, both be applied alternately. In Hayes's (2006) review of the research on freewriting, including the interactive study conducted by Galbraith and Torrence, the studies concur with the notion that it favours idea generation that leads to a more comprehensive understanding of the topic under consideration compared to other, more traditional organization-focused approaches, particularly because there seems to be less of a cognitive load on the writer from the outset.

How can technology favour freewriting practices? Here are some ideas in line within the QLL Dynamics framework:

1. The teacher provides a highly personalized topic for students to write about freely in their own time, using Microsoft Word or another more mobile-friendly app, such as James McMinn's *Writer*. Depending on the proficiency level, they can spend anywhere between 3 and 10 minutes.
2. The teacher holds a brief five-minute class discussion about the topic in class the next day.
3. Using their smartphones or tablets in class or going to the multimedia language lab, students write about the topic freely a second time. The time limits are the same as the night before.
4. In order to consolidate their understanding of the topic, students share their writings with other classmates and answer questions about what they wrote.
5. Students are then asked to write a third time, without referring to the original freewriting sample. The third time around, they follow the outline-based approach, using the original main ideas that have already been identified.
6. The teacher answers questions about writing conventions and the intended results.
7. Students do the work at home with Microsoft Word, using the spell checker to screen the contents and make certain the final form is deemed satisfactory for submission.

For more planned writing practice, there are a variety of alternatives. They include:

- *ESL Robot Pro*: For beginners, this app asks learners to type what they would like to say to the robot, which responds with an audible answer. This can be good practice at the phrase and sentence level because inaccurate statements will not be recognized.
- http://corpus.byu.edu: Brigham Young University offers a collection of corpora on its website, some of which are genre specific. The selections include the Wikipedia Corpus, Global Web-Based English Corpus, Corpus of Historical American English, Corpus of American Soap Operas, and the Time Magazine Corpus. General

corpora include links to the British National Corpus (BNC) and the Corpus of Contemporary American English (COCA). Although corpora have more of a vocabulary-learning focus in mind, the examples can help students make their writing more authentic.

- ww2.bubble.us and **freemind**.softonic.com: These apps help with the initial stage of the outline process by providing students with the means of creating mental maps or graphic organizers for their ideas on a particular topic. Students can move thought bubbles and enlarge the image, as well as save, share and print their maps.
- *English Writing Skills and Rules* (Top of Learning): This app for mobile devices provides flashcards with information, templates and models on how to write in response to diverse text types and genre, such as explanations, recounts, narratives, procedures, reports, essays, condolences and others.

Conclusion

In the end, reading and writing are essential skills without which English language proficiency development could not be complete. In fact, texts in the L2 are the main source through which new vocabulary is acquired, which, as we know, is decisive in determining the ceiling for both written and spoken expression. As stated earlier, writing is quickly becoming the preferred medium of communication for many situations and contexts commonly encountered in today's fast-paced world, where time to speak may be lacking or even undesirable. Rather than scorn 'texting', we should accept that it has become a 'written lingua franca of many youth today' (Vosloo, 2009, p. 2) and, I might add, of a great many adults as well. With technology as an invaluable resource and support, reading and writing skills can be learned, practised and consolidated far beyond what was once only possible in the classroom.

Discussion Questions

1. Why is it so important to integrate intensive and extensive reading in a study programme? How can it be done to ensure maximum learner participation?

2. What role do graded readers play in reading skill development? What would be one way to work with graded readers in a multimedia language lab?
3. Do texting, tweeting and posting for social media qualify as writing? Where are you in the debate as to whether social media do more harm or good for L2 writing?
4. How would you introduce technologically supported freewriting to your lessons?
5. Which do you prefer, planned or unplanned writing? How could you apply them in your class in a harmonious, mutually beneficial way?
6. What kind of feedback should teachers provide their students at different stages of the writing process? How can technology be used to help?

Suggested Readings

Grabe, W. (2009) *Reading in a Second Language: Moving from Theory to Practice* (Cambridge: Cambridge University Press).
Offers an extensive compilation of research, practical insights and ideas for exploratory practice related to reading.

Mercado, L. A. (2015) Chapter 19: 'Integrating Classroom Learning and Autonomous Learning', in D. Nunan and J. C. Richards (eds) *Language Learning beyond the Classroom* (New York: Routledge).
Offers more extensive detail on how to create an effective, technology-based intensive-extensive reading programme.

Plester, B., Wood, C., and Bell, V. (2008) 'Txt Msg n School Literacy: Does Texting and Knowledge of Text Abbreviations Adversely Affect Children's Literacy Attainment?' *Literacy*, 42(3), pp. 137–44.
Presents one of the few studies that addresses the issue of writing through social media.

CHAPTER 7

Language, Principles and Technology

> *The challenge ... is to design tasks that require learners to use inductive and deductive reasoning to develop their own understanding of the relationship between form and function.*
>
> Nunan, 1999a, p. 28

From an English language teaching perspective, the term 'language', as an object of study, is often construed to mean grammar. Over time, grammar has had different levels of notoriety within the field. With the grammar-translation method, for example, it was considered the cornerstone of the language learning process. But there have also been calls for diminishing and even eliminating its presence. Indeed, the role of grammar instruction in the second-language acquisition process has been highly questioned in the past (Krashen, 1982). Nevertheless, numerous research studies have since found that both classroom instruction and opportunities for communicative interaction using target forms can lead to grammatical acquisition (Ellis, 2006; Nunan, 1999b; Spada and Lightbrown, 2008). Consequently, the acquired language forms can be made available to the L2 user for communication in real-life situations, thus bestowing upon grammar learning a clearer sense of practical purpose.

Yet, form is much more than grammar. As Ellis (2001) reminds us, 'the term "form" is intended to include phonological, lexical, grammatical, and pragmalinguistic aspects of language' (p. 2). Vocabulary, for example, is extremely important because 'a small number of the words in English occur very frequently and if a learner knows these words, that learner will know a very large proportion of running words in written or spoken text' (Schmitt and McCarthy, 1997, p. 9). As for pronunciation, the correct articulation of sounds, as well as proper stress, intonation and rhythm, leads to greater comprehensibility of spoken language and thus contributes directly to effective communication; modern-day definitions for speaking fluency and proficiency development, for example, assign a great deal of importance to the intelligibility and comprehensibility of spoken language as opposed to the 'native-like' speech that was once expected in the past. Equally important, pragmalinguistics refers to the use of linguistic resources to perform practical communicative functions (Taguchi, Naganuma and Budding, 2015). For our discussion, this leads us to the following questions:

- What are the basic principles of grammar instruction to keep in mind when working with technology-based learning resources?
- How can grammar, pronunciation and vocabulary be learned more effectively through technology?
- How can technology facilitate the use of language forms in real-life situations?

Principles of Grammar Teaching

Despite the many methodological trends that have come into use over the years, there always seems to be a place for grammar. This is probably because, according to Celce-Murcia and Oshtain (2000), 'All languages have context-dependent options in grammar that enable speakers and writers to accomplish specific pragmatic and discourse forming functions' (p. 52). Today, if one were to review most publishers' course books for English language learning, one would probably find that they continue to have sections clearly dedicated to 'grammar'. However, it should never be taught in isolation or exempt from context. This is especially true if it is to serve a practical, communicative purpose. Reflecting on his extensive review of the research, Ellis (2006) offers the following list as essential considerations for teaching grammar:

1. Grammar instruction should highlight meaning and use as well as form.
2. Explicit grammar instruction should be called on for language forms that are known to be of high complexity, low frequency, and simply problematic.
3. Explicit grammar instruction will lead to better results when it is tied to communicative practice.
4. Formal instruction that promotes explicit knowledge on the part of learners can foster the acquisition of implicit knowledge as well.
5. Instruction that is likely to lead to the development of implicit knowledge will: (i) be extended over a period of time; and (ii) should be integrated with subsequent L2 input (e.g. structured, enhanced or even authentic)
6. Communicative tasks that require the use of a particular form for a successful performance (e.g. planned focus-on-form) may facilitate acquisition.

Regarding the first point on the list, Ellis refers to the three-dimensional framework Diane Larsen-Freeman (2003) has defined as *grammaring*. She cites its three pillars as being:

- Form: The visible or audible components of language as expressed through phonology, graphology/semiology, morphology and syntax. How is it constructed?
- Meaning: The semantics or meaning that is encoded in the language without contextualization. What does it mean?
- Use: The pragmatics or intended meaning of the language on the part of the user. When or why is it used?

From a general perspective, *form* and *meaning* may be suffi-cient to communicate a message in a comprehensible manner, but correct *use* is essential if that message is to be effective. Correct use allows for a proper understanding of the intended message and ensures appropriateness of the language for the situational context at hand.

In mainstream education, current positions on L1 grammar instruction seem at the very least interesting enough to consider. According to Navarre Cleary (2014), in a meta-analysis of over 250 studies dating from 1984 through 2012, traditional L1 grammar instruction was generally deemed less effective and at times even a hindrance to learning as opposed to approaches that placed a greater emphasis on learning grammar incidentally and upon need, particularly as learners engaged in writing and reading. In the case of writing, she argues that 'once students get ideas they care about onto the page, they are ready for instruction—including grammar instruction—that will help communicate those ideas'. Although this would seem to part from previously stated views in the field of second-language acquisition, the position is actually amenable to a certain degree. Teachers can incorporate rule discovery and information restructuring after the initial task of brainstorming or freewriting.

Form-Focused Instruction and Technology

Technology's role in form-focused instruction is to ensure extensive exposure to L2 forms. It can also make up for classroom limitations so that students have the opportunity to understand the forms they are learning and practice their use until acquisition is more likely to take place. Effective classroom grammar instruction will involve a well-versed teacher who can either explain the target form correctly when teaching deductively or facilitate the noticing process and subsequent understanding when having students work inductively. There should be visual and aural support as well as heavy emphasis on contextualizing the grammar as much as possible. The examples should be ample in scope and contextualized to the groups' schemata, improving comprehension of form, meaning and use as well as its application in both subsequent controlled practice and more open-ended communicative activities. In Figure 7.1, we see a graphic depiction that shows what teachers and others responsible for learning content and processes should consider to enhance the learning of forms:

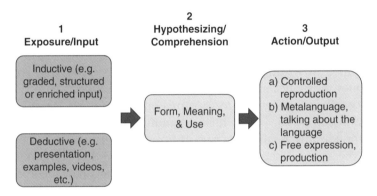

Figure 7.1 Cycle for learning forms in classroom and autonomous/flipped learning environments.

When planning a grammar lesson that uses technology, we must remember what we hope to accomplish with our students. Teachers who work with course books may realize that despite all of the talk of 'modern' approaches to grammar instruction, most publisher series still present a syllabus that appears, in one form or another, strongly oriented towards *mastery learning*. This is the instructional practice of presenting grammatical items one at time, practicing it until 'mastery' has been achieved and then moving on to the next item on the list (Bailey, 2005). Yet, we cannot expect all students to exhibit meaning-focused, spontaneous language production after a grammar presentation. What we can hope for at the very least is comprehension and reproduction of the language. Kelkar

(1978) describes *reproduction* as aimed at 'recapturing the reproducing user's reception of the original [utterance] … or at recapturing the production of the original' (p. 153); this is language that is controlled, semi-spontaneous, conscious, primarily form focused and accuracy oriented. In relation, teachers may unreasonably expect their students to engage in authentic language production almost as soon as new grammar is taught, which has clear negative implications for classroom and autonomous learning of grammar. With these points in mind, let us consider the following sample class, described in Table 7.1, according to the QLL Dynamics framework.

As for software, LMSs, MOOCs and apps, the principles for effective grammar instruction are the same. As Nunan (1999a) suggests, there should be an opportunity for students to see how form, meaning and use come together, and to understand their interrelationship, both deductively and inductively. Therefore, from an e-learning, technology-driven perspective, it is best for learning solution alternatives to offer what is normally done for diverse learning styles and preferences. Some alternatives are shown in Table 7.2:

ACTIVITY

Create a flipped lesson by choosing a grammatical structure from your course. Use or create your own blog site to upload content. Start with a video lesson by doing an Internet search on the terms 'English grammar' and 'video'. You will find a variety of options for video lectures on grammar, or you can create your own with the video camera on your PC/Mac or cell phone/tablet. Then follow the rest of the suggested 'flipped learning' sequence in the previous section to develop your presentation. Make sure to include slides that will prepare your students for their communicative practice in class.

Table 7.1 Sample Grammar Lesson Using Technology

	Deductive	Inductive
Exposure to Input	1. Teacher uses PowerPoint to show 'Present = am, is, are' and 'Past = was, were'. Teacher then shows examples with 'was/were' in which the position and form are highlighted as well as the supporting time clauses. Pictures support examples, such as 'Bill Clinton was the president of the United States from 1992 to 2000'; 'Iker Casillas was the goalie for Real Madrid until July 2015'; etc..	1. Teacher presents three words on the screen: 'past', 'present', and 'future'. Teacher asks students to associate each with one of the following words: 'nostalgia', 'today', and 'possible' (words can vary depending on context). Afterwards, students must match the items to one of the following years: 2001, 2017–18, or 2025.
Hypothesizing and Comprehension	2. Teacher then has students look at other pictures with correct and incorrect sentence formulations. Students must analyse and determine which use 'was/were' correctly. Limited but effective metalanguage should be encouraged for the discussion. Other practice activities are carried out using the IWB or regular board.	2. Teacher uses Prezi to show pictures and statements without making any initial remark except, 'Let's look at some new grammar.' The pictures should be accompanied by a sample text, with 'was/were' and a time clause. Teacher then has students work in groups to explain whether verbs are used in the past, present or future and what the form is for each subject; and to list examples of language that supports their conjectures.

Action and Output

3. Teacher has students brainstorm vocabulary related to people and places in order to create a pool of words that can feed into student-generated examples.

4. Students go to the lab to create their own slide shows in groups. They must use 'was/were' and visual support. The members of the group send their slideshows to themselves, the members of one other group and the teacher, so everyone reviews the content at home.

5. The next day, the teacher reviews the past tense by showing versions of the student-made presentations with no text. The presentations are identified by the group, so it must be students who did not make the highlighted presentation that come up with the statements. Students then practise using student-to-student questions for 'was/were', switching partners and seating arrangements.

Table 7.2 Modalities for Teaching Grammar According to the QLL Dynamics Framework and CALI

Learning modality	Technology	Instruction	Benefit
Deductive/controlled practice	English Grammar by Appsofindia: has explanations, examples and practice lessons for 28 different grammar structures. Grammar Up (www.grammar-express.com) and the British Council's Johnny Grammar app for mobile devices offer scored and gamified exercises.	Learners practice the target structure for the unit/course. They must come to class with their own examples and explanations. The teacher can have students do a surprise gamified exercise in the lab.	Students feel they are more in control of learning process, cognizant of their achievement and more accurate in their language production/ reproduction.
Metacognition/ feedback on grammar use	Applications for Macs and PCs, such as Grammarly, can help students identify, understand, and correct mistakes in their writing as they perform tasks.	With Grammarly, students can work on their writing. The feedback from the app can help initiate discussions with metalanguage. The feedback is available on an ongoing basis whenever they write on their computers or other devices.	Such apps provide metacognitive feedback to students automatically. Such feedback has been found in research to be beneficial to SLA.

Learning modality	Technology	Instruction	Benefit
Flipped learning	An LMS that offers grammar presentations, exercises, vocabulary and graded readers, such as Macmillan English Campus. There are also websites, such as learnertv.com, that offer lectures/presentations on grammar, vocabulary and pronunciation. Teachers can also create their own 'flipped' lessons.	Students watch the grammar presentations, which can be supported by videos and graded readers. In class, students role-play to demonstrate the use of the grammar for communication. Evaluations can be tied to flipped learning content in order to highlight the importance of studying the lesson at home.	The explicit content of the grammar lesson can be covered mostly at home, leaving time in class for clarification, additional not first-time practice and meaning-focused application. Students can review the content as many times as possible for full comprehension.
Structured and enriched input	Using Microsoft Publisher or specialized websites, such as www.storyjumper.com, pictures and content can be combined to create a variety of texts, highlighting the grammar or simply presenting numerous examples for noticing and analysis purposes.	The teacher can create stories, articles and other texts focusing on a specific grammar structure or vocabulary. Later, students can do the same as part of a project.	This modality of learning is more constructivist in nature, allowing students to engage in higher-order thinking skills as they create a unique product of their own.

Vocabulary

Vocabulary is perhaps what most establishes meaning and context in communication. It tells us the what, when, where, who and how of any given situation. It also conveys the intended scope of the context in communication, whether it is a reference to everyday personal activities and routines; the family and relationships; notions of community and society; or truly global issues and themes, such as global warming, international law and globalization. According to various international proficiency standards and benchmarks (e.g. ACTFL), communicative competence in response to such thematic domains serves as a prerequisite for determining degrees of proficiency development. From an SLA theory perspective, Douglas and Selinker's 'Discourse Domains' theory of interlanguage (1985) is heavily dependent on vocabulary because it aids in distinguishing levels of competency in the language according to context-setting themes and topics; for example, people who are well versed in music may seem highly proficient when using the L2 but much less capable and fluent when asked about sports or some other topic that is not of their general interest.

Because the importance of vocabulary is indisputable, what we must ascertain is how much vocabulary should be learned, when and how. Regarding the challenge of learning enough words for academic achievement in a higher education setting, Grabe and Stoller (2002) state:

> Unfortunately, we cannot teach students all of the words they need to know in a reasonable amount of time. Instead, we can focus on the 2,000 to 3,000 most common words as an essential foundation for word-recognition automaticity, and then focus on vocabulary that is appropriate to specific topics and fields of study. This ... requires a strong commitment to vocabulary instruction as an important component of reading development, and it is a view that many reading researchers now accept. The dilemma for teachers, then, is to teach vocabulary consistently and effectively, and how to get students to become collectors of words. (p. 79)

In his extensive review of the research, Schmitt (2008) confirms the need to have learners develop a large vocabulary, with knowledge requirements ranging from 2000–3000 word families at 95 per cent comprehension in order to understand spoken English and a range as high as 8000 to 9000 for authentic written texts. He also identifies a diverse mix of variables and prerequisite conditions that are necessary to foster systematic, long-lasting vocabulary learning in an instructional context. In relation, Schmitt's notion of 'maximizing engagement' refers to how anything that increases time, attention, manipulation and exposure in relation to new vocabulary is likely to promote its learning. In his review of his and other research, he highlights instructional strategies, lexis-focused activities and autonomous learning practices – all of which can be aided by technology – that can maximize vocabulary learning, as Table 7.3 summarizes.

The research of the past 25 years, summarized in Table 7.3, clearly indicates the need to develop language programmes and e-learning solutions with opportunities for incidental and autonomous learning, and multiple exposures to new vocabulary over time.

In order to maximize learners' exposure to new words, there are a number of alternatives, all of which should be integrated to maximize effect. In the classroom, teachers can present new words much as they would new grammar. With the aid of Power Point or Prezi, videos, **interactive white boards** and even the students' smartphones, words can be shown or looked up, discussed and worked on. Online dictionaries, e-books, graded readers and other texts can be sources of new words to identify and learn, or they can be used to create opportunities for additional exposures and further processing of partially learned words. As the research suggests, it is not enough to see new lexical items in the course book; students must also reflect on the words, see them several times, associate the words with their L1 equivalents when appropriate, support the words with imagery and sound, and manipulate and process the language through practice exercises and communicative tasks.

Table 7.3 Summary of Research Conclusions on the Learning of Vocabulary

Condition/ Practice	*Explanation*
Explicit and incidental learning	Opportunities for explicit instruction and incidental learning should be integrated in order to maximize effect.
Form, meaning and use	It is not enough to know the form and its meaning; when and how it should be used must also be understood if receptive vocabulary is to become productive in nature.
Form versus meaning	Form should be given as much importance as meaning, especially as research has found that learners tend to have the most problems with the first.
Multifaceted learning	Based on Nation's (2007) 'Four Strands' framework, there should be opportunities for meaning-focused input, meaning-focused output, language-focused learning and fluency development in the instructional cycle.
Incidental learning from reading and listening	There is a direct association between learning receptive and productive vocabulary and the number of exposures to new lexical items. Reading, especially of the extensive type, and guided listening tend to maximize incidental learning rates as opposed to simple exposure to L2 input.
Explicit instructional practice and learner training	Activities that focus on vocabulary explicitly in order to maximize attention, understanding and use, as well as those that follow up on incidental reading and listening acts, are likely to promote vocabulary learning and consolidation. These include post-reading and post-listening activities, glossing (cues for meaning in the margins of texts), guessing meaning from context, L2–L1 flash cards, constructive activities for practice and communication (e.g. collaborative output), etc..

The following sample learning path can take place in any language course – face-to-face, blended or fully online:

1. *Exposure to new words*: Students will be exposed to new words during the lesson. This can occur on the following occasions:
   a. Students will be exposed to L2 input in the form of texts for inductive learning and processing. A class discussion ensues.
   b. The teacher will explicitly teach new vocabulary.
   c. Words will be encountered in the course book and other study materials.
   d. Students will be asked to work with an online dictionary and thesaurus.
   e. Students will surf on the Internet to find examples.
2. *Identification of new words*: Students will be given time at different stages during the lesson to identify the new or partially familiar words they want to learn. There should be a target number per day as agreed by the teacher and the students in the class. These can be saved on their tablets or smartphones.
3. *Processing of new words*: Students will have the opportunity to process, practise and reflect on the new words they have chosen through a variety of means, including tasks and assignments in which students are to create oral and written language with the new words; practice exercises with multiple-choice, drag-and-drop, matching and other options; strategies for self-learning, such as word cards and vocabulary logs; freewriting activities; e-graded readers and other texts (e.g. articles); and so on.
4. *Assessment of learning*: Feedback can be immediate, as in the case of an LMS or other CALL media, or it can come later in the form of teacher-generated feedback, a quiz or test, or self-assessment techniques, such as recordings of one's performance in the use of the new vocabulary.
5. *Opportunities for L2 output*: In order to close the instructional/learning cycle (in class or online lesson), students will be given an opportunity to use the newly learned words in free, meaning-focused communicative activities, which will demonstrate their ability to use the words as productive vocabulary. They can also use metalanguage to explain the association between the item and its meaning in the L2, confirming it has been learned as receptive vocabulary; according to Nation (2008b), they can also

state the word after seeing its meaning in the L1, confirming its availability as productive vocabulary.

This instructional cycle can be particularly effective when technology is used in support. As an example, I have instituted this approach to vocabulary learning at the Euroidiomas language centre in Lima, Peru, with thousands of students and hundreds of teachers. Figure 7.2 shows a sample lesson on 'clothing items':

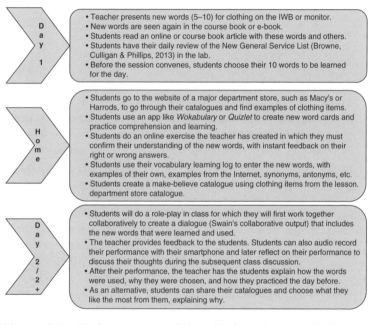

Day 1
- Teacher presents new words (5–10) for clothing on the IWB or monitor.
- New words are seen again in the course book or e-book.
- Students read an online or course book article with these words and others.
- Students have their daily review of the New General Service List (Browne, Culligan & Phillips, 2013) in the lab.
- Before the session convenes, students choose their 10 words to be learned for the day.

Home
- Students go to the website of a major department store, such as Macy's or Harrods, to go through their catalogues and find examples of clothing items.
- Students use an app like *Wokabulary* or *Quizlet* to create new word cards and practice comprehension and learning.
- Students do an online exercise the teacher has created in which they must confirm their understanding of the new words, with instant feedback on their right or wrong answers.
- Students use their vocabulary learning log to enter the new words, with examples of their own, examples from the Internet, synonyms, antonyms, etc.
- Students create a make-believe catalogue using clothing items from the lesson. department store catalogue.

Day 2/2+
- Students will do a role-play in class for which they will first work together collaboratively to create a dialogue (Swain's collaborative output) that includes the new words that were learned and used.
- The teacher provides feedback to the students. Students can also audio record their performance with their smartphone and later reflect on their performance to discuss their thoughts during the subsequent class discussion.
- After their performance, the teacher has the students explain how the words were used, why they were chosen, and how they practiced the day before.
- As an alternative, students can share their catalogues and choose what they like the most from them, explaining why.

Figure 7.2 Cycle over several days for learning vocabulary with technology.

As an extension, students can carry out a project during the course in which they must use a number of the newly learned vocabulary words. This can be written or performed in class as a speaking activity (e.g. presentation, role play, students teaching students, etc.). For assessment purposes, the words that were taught explicitly by the teacher can be included in quizzes and

ACTIVITY

Teach your students how to use word cards in class. Then have them create their own collection of word cards, using apps like Wokabulary, Quizlet or any other. Identify a pool of 400 words that are pertinent to the course and make it a goal for them to learn at least 50 of those words a week by using word cards. At the end of the 8 weeks, have them take an assessment for receptive and productive vocabulary. How many words did they actually learn?

tests to ensure that students understand their importance for the course. Students can also engage in extensive reading by using a library of online graded readers and working with the new words on their own after getting some special training from the teacher.

It is important for there to be daily targets for learning. With 10 new words per day in a 17-days-a-month course, students can potentially learn more than 2000 words a year, not including those words students may choose to learn on their own. It is also important to train students on how they can cultivate vocabulary learning outside of class. The use of word cards, for example, is perhaps one of the most effective means for learning a large number of words in a very short period of time, with retention and recall rates remaining mostly the same for a very long time (Nation, 2008b). Dr Charles Browne, Dr Brent Culligan and Joseph Phillips have created the New General Service List (NGSL) (http://www.newgeneralservicelist.org), which compiles the 2800+ most frequent words in the English language; it is an updated version of Michael West's 1953 General Service List (GSL). By going to the website, teachers will find *Quizlet* word cards for all of the words. They are presented in cohorts of 50, so they can be learned by students a few at a time.

An application like *Wokabulary* can help students create their own word cards as they identify new words each day. Students can enter the word, its genre or category name and even the speaker's L1 as a means of identifying. The application shows the new word in the L2, and students can turn it around to see its description or definition in the L1. Students can even import previously made lists that the application makes available according to word family and genre. As students work with the app, it identifies those words which are most easily identified and those they are having more problems with, which are then recycled and emphasized in subsequent quizzes. Of course, students can construct their own word card library, using something as simple as PowerPoint, with words, pictures, audio and even video to support the 'cards' they make. Eventually, learners may be able to reach new thresholds for vocabulary surpassing those we may have seen in the past.

In Chapter 4, we saw how the *Let's Speak* lesson for guiding live interactive sessions online has a communicative focus. There is also a version with a grammatical and vocabulary-centred focus. It is designed to get students to speak, but rather than prioritize meaning-focused communication between the online tutor and the student, it is more geared towards getting the student to use metalanguage and engage in speaking practice for fluency rate-building or other explicit training techniques. Figure 7.3 shows some screen shots.

ACTIVITY

Valeria Guerra and William Machado are teachers in Montevideo, Uruguay. In their classes, they elect a student to be the 'Star of the Week', who uploads to the class wiki six new words for the week. The other students must write a sentence for these new words in the fields to the right. Words cannot be repeated, and students must do some research first before posting their sentences. The next week, a new 'Star of the Week' is chosen, and the process begins again. Create your own wiki and have students do this activity. Did they find it helpful?

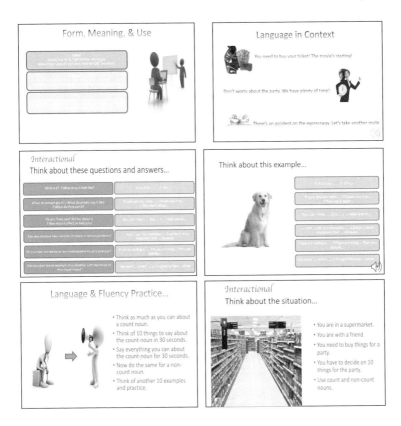

Figure 7.3 *Let's Speak* slides to support online videoconferencing.

Pronunciation

Pronunciation is an aspect of English language teaching that teachers may be least comfortable with. There may be a tendency to cover the course book's activity for pronunciation quickly and move on to the next activity. While presenting the content, teachers may also limit examples of the pronunciation feature to those presented in the course book. Actually, this happens either because they are not well-versed enough in their knowledge of phonetics or '[w]hen they do find the time to address pronunciation, the instruction often amounts to the presentation and practice of a series of tedious and seemingly unrelated topics' (Gilbert, 2008, p. 1). Nevertheless, without pronunciation practice and the achievement of acceptable levels of intelligibility, a learner's speech may not be fluent or comprehensible, having direct implications for effective communication.

As stated in Chapter 5, an important aspect of L2 proficiency in speaking is fluency during communicative interaction. Research studies have considered measures in speech rate, automaticity, use of discourse markers and language chunks, and turn-taking as means of determining the degree of fluency development in spoken English (McCarthy, 2010). Interestingly enough, studies in other fields, particularly speech pathology and psychology, have shown that pronunciation practice can contribute to improving the sound articulations – at the segmental and suprasegmental level - most associated with attaining fluent speech. Moreover, computer-mediated cognitive behaviour therapies have been found to be quite effective for improving speech fluency in persons with speech impairments (Iverach and Rapee, 2014; Packman, 2012). The apparent implications are that in addition to the virtues of pronunciation practice that are widely recognized in the field of ESL/EFL, other fields concur with its importance in promoting effective, fluent oral communication.

Technology has an important role to play because it can provide learners with the means to practice pronunciation on their own and in the place of their choosing. This takes on an additional significance when one is reminded of the hesitation in many teachers to dedicate sufficient time to pronunciation practice in the classroom. Computer-mediated, mobile-accessible pronunciation practice can offer some advantages that could make it more engaging for learners to carry it out as opposed to traditional classroom techniques and exercises. First of all, learners are in control, so they decide what they want to practice and for how long. Additionally, pronunciation activities are generally supported by graphics, images, and animations. But perhaps the most important feature is the ability on the part of learners to self-assess by comparing their utterances with samples of the target language. They can also receive automatic feedback in the form of a spectrograph or – more recently – scored analyses of segmental and suprasegmental sound reproductions. *ELL Technologies*, for example, has a pronunciation tool called 'The Studio', which looks like an actual sound studio on the screen; it analyzes and scores the learner's ability to say three- to four-word collocations at the individual sound level, highlighting the specific sounds which need to be improved and not just the person's stress, rhythm and intonation. It could be argued that this kind and amount of feedback would be more difficult for learners to obtain in a regular classroom setting. Here are some additional examples of apps that can help a learner practice pronunciation:

- *Sounds: The Pronunciation App* (Adrian Underhill, Macmillan): The free version for mobile devices provides learners with an interactive phonemic chart. Students can press on the phonemic symbol to hear the sound and an example of a word with the sound, match words with their phonetic spellings, phonetically spell the word that appears or listen to a word and spell it phonetically. The premium version expands the options significantly to include a list with 650 words; the ability to choose specific phonemes so that the exercises can focus on them for practice; timed and game-like quizzes; and practical tips for teachers and students.
- *Æ English Pronunciation*: This free app provides opportunities to listen to vowel and consonant sounds, listen to sample words, record your repetition of sample words, practise phonetic spellings and work with an interactive phonemic chart, among other features. There also images and videos to help with the articulation of the sounds.
- *How to Speak English*, by Kaplan: This free app focuses on those sounds that are difficult for learners, depending on their L1 background. It provides videos of how the sounds and words should be produced as well as audio samples of phonemes and sample words. As the person in the video is modelling the sound and manipulating the speech organs, learners can video record themselves as they are repeating. The video file is saved on a mobile device.

ACTIVITY

After doing some preliminary work with a specific segmental or suprasegmental feature, divide the class into two. Have one group practice on their own, using apps that highlight the speech organs in videos and other media, while the second continues the course without such support. This can be done in the lab as well. Establish a set number of hours of practice per week. After two weeks, conduct an assessment. Which group does a better job with the sound or feature being taught?

These apps and others serve multiple purposes that are conducive to improving one's ability to pronounce English words and phrases correctly. They all reinforce a learner's auditory discrimination, which is the ability to identify and distinguish between phonemes or individual sounds as well as similar and dissimilar words (Kuczynski and Kolakowsky-Hayner, 2011). With apps that allow learners to record and playback their own production of a model utterance, the purpose is to improve their internal auditory discrimination, or the awareness of how one produces sounds her- or himself; this allows learners to compare their utterance to the model and determine the extent to which they are similar, thus providing a criterion for successful pronunciation and general comprehensibility. Effective external auditory discrimination is required before internal auditory discrimination is possible (Dale, 2012), which means that learners must be able to understand correctly how the word 'sheep' is pronounced before they are able to determine if they are pronouncing it correctly themselves. Overall, using the QLL Dynamics framework within the application of CALI, a typical lesson for pronunciation practice could be as follows:

1. The teacher uses an app in the classroom, like the University of Iowa's *Sounds of Speech*, or a YouTube video to show students an animated depiction of the speech organs/articulators as a specific

sound – the focus of the lesson – is made. The same could be done in a multimedia language lab on a more personalized basis. Students practise chorally and in pairs, switching partners while circulating in the classroom when a specific number of turns has been completed.

2. At home or any other place of their choosing, students can record their voices using their smartphones or PC/Mac-based voice recorder and then send the samples to their teacher by way of Messenger, Whatsapp, email or Skype, for formative assessment or grading purposes.

3. Teachers can help their students create a record of their progress in learning how to pronounce difficult words through an e-portfolio, with recordings and journal entries that can be stored over time.

Conclusion

This chapter addressed the essential foundations of teaching and learning forms through technology. More importantly, the CALI was exemplified with practical examples of how to initiate the learning cycle in class; have learners continue developing their knowledge and practice of target forms on their own; and ultimately demonstrate their ability to apply what they have learned for communication once they have returned. Not only is this a practical approach to ensuring greater learning but also one that is strongly grounded in research.

Discussion Questions

1. What are some ways in which we can use technology to facilitate the inductive learning of forms? Can learners use a simple cell phone for the task?

2. How would you present a grammar point in a setting with limited resources, without technology in the classroom and a limited number of computers in the multimedia language lab?

3. How would you use the General Service List (GSL) or New General Service List (NGSL) to inform your teaching of vocabulary through technology? How could your students do the same when learning on their own?
4. What does research seem to say about the incidental learning of vocabulary as opposed to explicit instruction? How would you use online graded readers to promote both?
5. Why is having learners who listen to their own pronunciation of words, phrases and sentences so important? How could they send samples of their pronunciation practice to you?
6. How would you organize a three- or four-minute flipped video lesson on a pronunciation feature?

Suggested Readings

Ellis, R. (2006) 'Current Issues in the Teaching of Grammar: An SLA Perspective', *TESOL Quarterly*, 40(1), pp. 83–107.
Although published sometime ago, this article presents everything a teacher needs to know about grammar instruction.

Nation, I.S.P. (2008) *Teaching Vocabulary: Strategies and Techniques.* (Boston, MA: Heinle Cengage Learning).
As with Ellis's article, Nation's book is a requirement for anyone who wishes to understand vocabulary learning.

Schmidt, N. (2008) 'Instructed Second Language Vocabulary Learning', *Language Teaching Research*, 12(3), pp. 329–63.
Another authority whose work can be highly enlightening on when and how to learn vocabulary.

Underhill, A. (2005). *Sound Foundations: Learning and Teaching Pronunciation* (New York: Macmillan).
Leads to a better understanding of pronunciation as a whole and also provides insights on how to make good use of Underhill's excellent app.

8 Technology for Assessment, Evaluation and Proficiency Testing

Advances in technology should encourage test developers to move beyond the thinking that has long dominated paper-and-pencil testing and inspire the use of 'disruptive' applications, by which assessments are conceptualized and implemented in innovatively different ways.

Chalhoub-Deville, 2001, p. 97

To this day, Chalhoub-Deville's quote may be right on the mark when it refers to the need to find new ways of conducting assessment through technology. At times, however, it may seem difficult for some to part with tradition, and the possible reasons are many. Reviewing the literature for ELT classroom practitioners, assessment appears to be an area for which there are significantly fewer publications as compared to other topics and issues. This may be because assessment is no easy task and is one which requires a distinctly high level of knowledge and expertise from teachers because of its complexity and potential implications, especially in high-stakes situations. Consequently, the lack of literature on the subject may hinder innovative thinking, which brings another issue to bear: teacher literacy in assessment. As Popham (2009) points out, 'Many of today's teachers know little about educational assessment. For some teachers, *test* is a four-letter word, both literally and figuratively. … Regrettably, when most of today's teachers completed their teacher-education programmes, there was no requirement that they learn anything about educational assessment' (p. 5). This chapter provides an array of references, insights and practical examples that support successful assessment practice, using technology as a vital resource in the classroom and beyond. Some questions we can think about include these:

- How can technology facilitate assessment of our students' language skills in ways that are effective and innovatively different?
- How can technology encourage our students to engage in self-assessment?
- Can technology promote reflection among learners on progress and achievement?
- How can technology foster and validate progression in our students' language proficiency development over time?

Assessment serves the purpose of confirming, to varying degrees, whether students are learning. In order to ascertain levels of progress and achievement, a language programme should have clearly identified goals, objectives, planned outcomes and standards against which learner performance can be gauged. Assessment can also take place at any time. As a tool and resource, technology can facilitate a teacher's ability to carry out assessment more effectively. It can make assessment applicable to more than one venue. Where it can make a great impact is in serving as a means of providing non-traditional, highly engaging input to stimulate learner responses, which can then be evaluated. The technological tool or resource can also serve to collect and save data, such as language samples, artefacts or other measures of progress and performance, for reference at any time. Another preferred feature is that it should facilitate the categorization of learner data so that it reflects degrees of achievement or performance. Equally important is its role in making the assessment process simpler and more efficient, reducing the amount of time and effort required on the part of the key stakeholders. Finally, decision-makers should be able to rely on the information and conclusions obtained from using a specific technology. Ideally then, a specific technological alternative should provide one or more of the following conditions for successful application of technology to assessment (Figure 8.1):

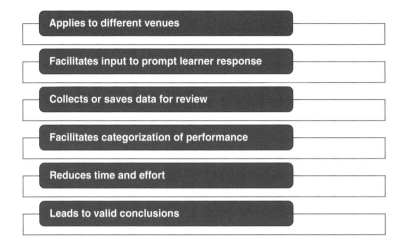

Figure 8.1 Conditions for successful application of technology to assessment.

In today's typical classroom, assessment and evaluation (for grading) are still more likely to be done in a traditional manner. Teachers collect data from their students and then assess language samples or other types of information related to performance. In doing so, teachers often resort to the use of note-taking and form-filling in order to have a record of what took place. Of course, formative assessment also takes place without the use of written records; teachers assess the input they receive from their students as they interact throughout the lesson, and make decisions or judgements based on how well they think the students are learning. This is often the result of what Schön (1983) calls 'reflection-in-action', which is when teachers make decisions as they engage in on-the-spot reflection in relation to what they are seeing and what their students are doing, especially when there are 'surprises, pleasing and promising or unwanted' (p. 56). In fact, research in general shows that teachers may make as many as 200–300 decisions in an hour during a typical lesson (Froschauer and Bigelow, 2012), with perhaps a majority of these being made as assessment is taking place. In relation, Brookhart (1997) points out:

Teachers are always observing their students informally. Teachers watch student behavior, academic work, and interpersonal interactions. They look for work habits, for evidence of conceptions and misconceptions about the various topics of instruction, for evidence of interest or lack of it, and for consistencies or changes in behavior. They interpret all this evidence in an ongoing manner …Various studies have estimated that teachers spend one-third to one-half of their professional time engaged in either formal or informal assessment activities and make literally hundreds of educational decisions per hour based on this evidence (p. 3).

The key issue is to make sure that the data is collected in sufficient amounts, at opportune moments, and acted on or used quickly and effectively.

Eliciting Learner Responses

Before we can engage in assessment and evaluation, we must elicit learner responses, which can take many forms depending on the language skill or knowledge area that is being addressed. Certainly, for activities and tasks to work, they must include effective prompts, which can take the form of pictures, texts, sounds, or audios and videos of various lengths. As opposed to what we would find in the more traditional classroom, which depended greatly on the board, visual aids in the form of flashcards, and teacher instructions, technology affords us a greater array of effective alternatives, as the following example suggests (Figure 8.2): Which of these celebrities do you dislike the most? Why?

Figure 8.2 Sample activity using Microsoft PowerPoint to elicit learner speaking or writing.

With Microsoft PowerPoint and a large screen, teachers can simply put together a slide with the information above and show it to students. In fact, in order to favour the shy and weaker students, a sample video can be made available on the institutional intranet in order to provide instructions on how the activity is to be carried out as well as footage of other students – with their permission – modelling what they will be expected to do the next day. In the example above, the teacher is supposed to project the images of five different, potentially unlikeable celebrities as well as a guiding question. Making such a slide takes much less time and is less expensive than creating traditional flashcards and writing the information on the board. Using PowerPoint also makes it adaptable, so the celebrities and the discussion question can be changed depending on the group or context. Linguistically speaking, the lesson above could be used to have students practice the use of adjectives associated with personality traits, or it may be used to promote fluency if it is timed; coupled with a cooperative learning technique, such as timed-pair-share or Round Robin, STT can be made extensive and equal for all of the students. Because it is using a technological medium, it can be saved for future use with other groups taking the same course. It can also be used as a prompt for a writing activity.

I have used this activity before, with examples of Peruvian celebrities from what is locally called *Chollywood*, a satirical reference to the local version of 'Hollywood'. I chose them carefully so the task would be appealing to any gender; the students would be able to say a great deal about each one because they were so familiar. Images were captured and pasted from Google images. The use of Microsoft PowerPoint saved me a great deal of time and helped make the activity more engaging through the use of visual supports that were highly appealing and effective in bringing about strong emotions. Table 8.1 provides some other examples of lessons for the different skills that use technology to introduce content and prompts:

Table 8.1 Uses of Technology to Assess Student Language Skills and Knowledge

Skill/Focus Area	L2/Instructional Input	Assessment with Technology
Reading	Graded readers or authentic readings that have been graded and vetted by teachers	Students record themselves under timed conditions with their smartphones or tablets as they work on reading fluency and then send the files to their teacher for assessment and feedback. They can also assess themselves with an appropriate teacher-created instrument to guide them.
Listening	YouTube or TedTalks videos, podcasts, audios from the course book, songs	A content management platform, such as Moodle, can be used to store the content and deliver it to the students, as well as provide the assessment for immediate correction and feedback. It is perhaps easier if the questions are made using test generator software, such as those that come with the content management platform, the course book materials, or an app with similar capabilities.
Writing	A writing task supported by pictures or video.	The writing task can be presented through the institutional Intranet, the teacher's blog or website, or a learning management system (LMS). Some LMSs now come with auto-correct technology, so students can get feedback from the computer. Of course, teachers can augment the information with feedback of their own.

Formative Assessment	Simple quiz with questions related to a language or lesson point that ask them directly how much they think they understand.	Teachers can use *Socrative* or a similar app to administer on-the-spot formative quizzes, which can be taken on a mobile phone or in the classroom or multimedia language lab. Such information can serve to identify whether more review is required or if it is time to move on.
Life Skills	An image depicting a situation in an academic or professional setting	Students can role-play a negotiation, for example, between an employee who is being laid off and a human resources supervisor or manager, recording their performances on a tablet, uploading the footage to a cloud (virtual storage on the Internet) and sharing it with the teacher so the video can be watched in class and discussed. Feedback can be provided by the teacher electronically and in person.

ACTIVITY

Try to identify at least three types of information you normally collect in class when carrying out formative assessment. Then use a form of technology to help you with at least one of them. Was it helpful?

Collecting and Saving Data

As stated earlier, assessment allows us to determine how much our students are learning at any given time. In the case of formative, non-graded assessment, decisions are often made on the spot and do not require the teacher to save data for later reference. In other cases, however, the language samples and the assessment/evaluation data need to be collected and stored, especially if grading decisions are in order, and the highest degree of accuracy and objectivity are to be ensured. In the case of language samples, they can be stored for later access by the teacher or – better yet – students using a wide variety of alternatives, including blogs, wikis, social media, content management platforms (e.g. Moodle, Blackboard), apps (e.g. Pinterest, Tumblr), smartphone audio and video files, clouds and others.

In the case of learner speaking, particularly during classroom activities and tasks, it is essential for the teacher to listen carefully to the students' samples and determine to what extent the language they produce meets pre-established criteria for achievement and success. The constructs, which are the characteristics of the knowledge, skill or ability to be measured (e.g. fluency, accuracy, pronunciation, comprehensibility, etc.) must be clearly defined in the mind of the teacher, the student and all of the other stakeholders who may need the information at some point or another. The scoring procedure must also be simple and teacher-friendly, meaning that it allows for a quick assignment of a score once the teacher has finished listening to the language sample and processing it. Amazingly, this process of listening, evaluating, and deciding on a grade takes place within a matter of seconds, unless, of course, the teacher wishes to record the sample and grade it later. Oftentimes, the teacher must evaluate one student and then move on to the next one, until all 15, 20, 25 or even more students have received a grade. This is easier said than done, of course. The assessment cycle depicted graphically in Figure 8.3 clearly demonstrates the steps that teachers often follow:

Figure 8.3   Assessment/evaluation cycle for speaking.

Technology can help enormously with this process. Performance descriptors could be made readily available on a smartphone or tablet so that teachers could listen to the sample and immediately categorize it using the rubric that has been chosen for the activity or task. This makes it easier for teachers to associate the language sample to a level of performance, which would be visible on the device at the moment of evaluation. This would also make the process more objective as the teacher would cross reference the sample with the respective performance descriptor rather than rely on subjective criteria found in one's mind that may not be as accurately remembered. *AllforRubrics*, for example, is a free app that allows teachers to create their own class rosters, rubrics, checklists and badges in order to categorize learner performance. Teachers can call on a specific rubric for a language skill, project or any

ACTIVITY

Plan a lesson that includes the use of mobile phones as a source of prompts for speaking assessment. Include voice recordings as part of the assessment process.

other task or activity, depending on the learning goal and objective, and select the box with the score and descriptor that match the quality of the student's language sample. It automatically scores it according to the preset criteria the teacher created and saves the information for future reference. Teachers can write their own objectives or intended learning outcomes as well as their corresponding 'can do' descriptors. They can also create what the app calls 'checklists' for a more holistic or formative assessment as well as 'badges' to serve as further recognition of accomplishment. Figure 8.4 gives an example of a rubric for basic-level students that I created using the *AllforRubrics* app:

Items	Beginning (1 Point)	Developing (2 Points)	Accomplished (3 Points)	Exemplary (4 Points)
To order food in a restaurant, using "will have" or "would like" Score = 3/4	The student can indicate a food item or drink for an order, using a short, incomplete statement.	The student can indicate a food item or drink for an order, using a short, complete statement with "will have" or "would like".	The student can order food items and drinks, using complete statements with 'will have' and 'would like'.	The student can ask about and order food items and drinks, using elaborated questions and statements with 'will have' and 'would like'.

Edit *Print* *Done*

Figure 8.4 Rubric item created for a basic-level course using *AllforRubrics* app.

It is also possible to record student speech for later assessment and grading. Smartphones and tablets both come with their own microphones and recording features. As students are performing, the teacher can place the device or its respective microphone (on the headset) either closer to the student if it is a pair work activity or in the middle of a group that is working together. Here are some examples of other apps that facilitate content storage and sharing on the part of both teachers and students:

- *Edmodo* is a virtual classroom that allows students and teachers to exchange a variety of content, including messages, posts for discussion forums, feedback on assignments, presentations, videos, sound files, pictures and others. Teachers can add content to share by storing it in the 'Library' while students have their own 'Backpack' for the content they wish to upload and share.
- *Pinterest*, as a social media website, allows students to post images of all kinds and personalize the content by adding their own comments, which is the equivalent of having their own collections.
- *Tumblr* serves as a platform for personal blogs, allowing users to post all kinds of texts, pictures and other images, audios, videos and links.

These and other apps allow teachers a look at what their students can produce and how it comes to represent their knowledge, skills and competencies. Accordingly, they can assess and evaluate their students' progress and achievements over time.

Learner portfolios have long been a subject of praise in the educational field. They represent a powerful means of alternative assessment that parts from traditional testing to offer both teachers and learners the opportunity to access a more holistic and representative view of how learning has taken place. Specifically, a learner portfolio:

> contains work that a learner has collected, reflected upon, selected, and presented to show growth and change over time, work that represents an individual's ... human capital. A critical component of an educational portfolio is the learner's reflection on the individual pieces of work (often called *artefacts*) as well as an overall reflection on the story that the portfolio tells about the learner.' (Barrett, 2007, p. 446)

In their review of research studies related to diverse modalities of reflective learning and learner portfolios, Davies and Le

Mahieu (2003) found that in general learning based on learner choice, ownership and action on reflection – the staples of learner portfolios – often lead to increased levels of motivation, autonomy, awareness of progress and overall achievement on the part of learners. This makes a great deal of sense when one considers that with portfolios an important part of the learning process is truly personalized, with learners choosing what they want to share and what may best represent their accomplishments. As Davies and Le Mahieu explain, 'Giving students choices about what to focus on next in their learning, opportunities to consider how to provide evidence of their learning (to show what they know), and to reflect on and record the learning the evidence represents makes it more possible to learn successfully' (p. 9).

E-portfolios are the technological next step to classroom portfolios. They provide a wide range of advantages in that they can be saved and stored indefinitely, make it easier to access and share the contents, and allow for more diverse and varied content (e.g. texts, audio, video, presentations, etc.). Barrett (2007) suggests that learners should not only carefully choose the contents for their e-portfolios as evidence of their learning, but that they also include a rationale for how each artefact represents the accomplishment of specific learning goals, objectives, outcomes or standards.

Recently, I included the promotion and use of e-portfolios as a vital component of a blended English study programme that *Euroidiomas* – my current institution – would offer a very large Latin American university. The idea is centred on offering students the opportunity to choose samples of their work for inclusion in an e-portfolio that is supposed to represent their progress over time as well as their ultimate achievements at the end of each course level in the programme (e.g. A1, A2, B1 according to the CEFR). The samples can be Word or PowerPoint documents, pictures with captions, audios, videos or any other type of media they feel is representative of their skills in the language. Students are expected to include artefacts that show where they began, their progress over time, and ultimately what they were able to achieve by the time they completed each level in the study programme. The programme includes an induction on what e-portfolios are, the benefits they offer students, how they are created, what they are supposed to include and how students can share the contents with their classmates, instructors and other stakeholders, including potential employers. At present, we at Euroidiomas plan to integrate e-portfolios in a new nationwide e-learning training program for English teachers that is being carried out on behalf of the Ministry of Education. In Table 8.2, we summarize an innovative example of e-portfolios being used at Centro Cultural Colombo Americano, an important binational centre in Cali, Colombia, as stated by Brayan Portilla Quintero, the teacher:

At the classroom level, teachers and students can make use of an existing app. *Pathbrite*, for example, is free and provides all of the features that an e-portfolio should have. It allows students and teachers to upload a variety of artefacts, which can be shared by sending the link by e-mail to classmates, the teacher or anyone the owner of the e-portfolio chooses. There is also the option to share it by way of the owner's LinkedIn, Facebook or Twitter account. The sharing feature is particularly useful and may even prove crucial when dealing with potential employers or encountering opportunities for academic advancement or professional development.

E-portfolios can serve as an ideal catalyst for learner motivation by making learners more aware of how their efforts can lead to tangible outcomes and benefits. We should remember from our discussion in Chapter 2 that amotivation and subsequent disenchantment with language learning can set in if learners cannot perceive a clear relationship between their efforts and what they consider to be acceptable outcomes (Vandergrift, 2005). E-portfolios are therefore an excellent means to maintain learner motivation from the beginning of a learning experience to its culmination. Bandura's self-efficacy theory, for example, is strongly grounded in learner perceptions of

Table 8.2   Activity for Having Students Create Their Own e-Portfolios

Name of Activity	Raising Students' Learning Awareness through E-Portfolios
Goal	Foster students' reflection and awareness towards the learning process through an e-portfolio that uses the Dropbox cloud storage platform.
CEFR Levels	B1–B1+
Procedure: Step 1	The teacher designed a *calendar of activities* for a one-and-a-half-month course period. The activities included entries that students were to save in their personal e-Portfolio Learning Log file (opinions and short descriptions, research, video searches and reflections, image and article readings, and test preparation reflections.)
Procedure: Step 2	The teacher surveyed students on their knowledge of technological tools and then presented the main objectives of the use of the e-portfolios in class. Students then received training on how to use Dropbox.
Procedure: Step 3	The teacher created individual folders for each student in his or her Dropbox account, with a file called 'Learning Log' that allowed students to save their course work. The teacher had an active role in providing feedback. In addition, a weekly review of each student's e-portfolio and Learning Log helped the teacher keep track of students' work and awareness.
Procedure: Step 4	After conducting all the activities, the teacher included two more files for each student's e-portfolio, a *self-check activity* to ensure learning log completeness and a *self-evaluation rubric* designed to allow students to express their perception about their own e-portfolio in terms of language learning awareness.
Procedure: Step 5	The teacher informed students about the results of the project. Students openly discussed their impressions as the teacher shared some of the opinions and reflections they had had about using e-portfolios in class.

their own achievement as well as those of similar others, such as their classmates. By definition, 'expectations of personal efficacy determine whether coping behavior will be initiated, how much effort will be expended, and how long it will be sustained in the face of obstacles and aversive experiences' (Bandura, 1977, p. 191). Schunk (1991) further explains, 'Individuals who feel efficacious are hypothesized to work harder and persist longer when they encounter difficulties than those who doubt their capabilities' (p. 207). As students see their progress and ever-growing abilities in the language, they should have a stronger motivation to work harder and achieve ever-higher goals. Schunk provides us with an additional insight: 'An individual also acquires capability information from knowledge of others. Similar others offer the best basis for comparison … Observing similar peers perform a task conveys to observers that they too are capable of accomplishing it' (p. 208). This essentially means that with e-portfolio sharing, learners can reinforce their self-concepts and see the work and progress of others as a powerful incentive to meet their own goals.

At the institutional level, existing content management platforms can be adapted to facilitate the collection of e-portfolios. In the case of Moodle, for example, there are several plug-ins, or applications that can be embedded in and integrated with the platform, that facilitate the creation and use of e-portfolios, including *SPDC Portfolio, Exabis* and *Mahara.*

ACTIVITY

Have your students create and use an e-portfolio after providing the necessary introduction and orientation. What kinds of artefacts do they collect, and what is their rationale for including them?

Assessment and Standards

In principle, all language programmes seek to maximize student learning. Yet learning a second language is a highly complex process, and meticulous planning does not always lead to expected results. In Latin America, for example, efforts have been made to promote English language learning on scales never seen before, and some of these initiatives have even led to ambitious national bilingual programmes. Unfortunately, in some cases, such as in Colombia and Chile, there has been little or no progress in terms of overall language proficiency development on the part of students in the public education system despite incessant efforts since 2000 and seemingly well-designed programmes (Cely, 2015; Government of Chile, 2014). Nevertheless, in spite of these and other setbacks, new national programmes, goals and strategies are being implemented in the region. Colombia and Chile have re-launched their programmes, and Peru just started implementing its own *National English Plan: Doors to the World* in 2015; in order to help the country's youth become global citizens, the Peruvian government seeks to have them attain a consolidated intermediate level of proficiency in English by the country's bicentennial in 2021, relying on a significant contribution from new technologies to facilitate achievement of this goal. The strategy combines the use of innovative, technology-based learning solutions and an increase in the number of hours of classroom instruction per week to achieve greater learning on the part of students. The *Aulas 1000* (*Thousand Classrooms*) programme, for example, benefits 3500 English teachers and 345,000 secondary students nationwide who are using online and offline platforms to develop their language and teaching skills, respectively (Acurio, as cited by the Peruvian Ministry of Education, 2015). Uruguay is another example of innovative language learning and assessment with its *Plan Ceibal Inglés* (*English Ceibal Plan*), which integrates videoconferencing between language instructors who are in a distant location and teachers and students in a classroom. The programme includes technologically supported assessment. It has already reached 600 schools in the country, with a current potential network of 1300 (Presidency of Uruguay, 2015).

Ideally, language programmes for learners in the public or private sector will be well designed and lead to tangible outcomes. According to my Quality Learning formula, introduced in Chapter 2, it would be best if international proficiency tests were integrated with language programmes in some manner, as they can serve as an objective means of confirming a learner's proficiency development. As a means of assessment, they maximize actual learning because of their ability to measure specific skills and competencies in the language and they also do the same for perceived learning because students become cognizant of their progress and overall achievement once they receive their certificates from the respective international testing agency. In the language programmes I have directed, I have always introduced a range of international proficiency tests to be taken by students at different stages in the learning process, offering tens of thousands of students – from young children to working adults – the opportunity to take them at no cost and to receive their exam certificates as a validation of their learning. What I can say is that high achievement on these tests or examinations requires a robust language programme whose principal focus is on 'good learning' rather than explicit test preparation.

Rather than 'teach to the test', what can be done is to provide e-learning tools and resources that can indirectly prepare students for the proficiency tests they may be taking later on. In other words, as students are taking their courses at different instructional levels, it may be advisable to have them practice with contents that will familiarize them with the kinds of questions, instructions, time constraints and overall formatting considerations that they will encounter at some point when the time comes to take an international proficiency test. With what I call **international test familiarization**, the 'challenge is to optimize the students' chances of performing well on their respective examinations without making the programme too test-preparation oriented' (Mercado, 2015a, p. 176). In my experience over the past four years, the following statistics describe the levels of achievement on international proficiency examinations for thousands of students:

- Of those who completed at least 300 hours of instruction, 100 per cent of them reached a B1 level of proficiency.
- Of those who completed at least 600 hours of instruction, more than 85 per cent reached a B2 level of proficiency.

The overall success of the language programmes was evident and consistent, with information that was derived from the monthly statistical reports and compiled over time. I would say that these encouraging results could be attributed in part to the students' ongoing use of e-learning resources to complement what they were learning in the classroom, including international test familiarization materials. According to institutional studies that were carried out under my direction on different occasions between 2006 and 2013, as many as 69 per cent of the students used their LMS and other e-learning resources (e.g. e-readers, online exercises, e-books, etc.) regularly, accessing them at least three times a week and averaging two hours of autonomous work during the same period. For such international test familiarization, technology-based resources (e.g. LMSs), here are some key considerations:

- Include question items that resemble those on international proficiency exams in terms of length, content type and format.
- Time exercise or task completion in order to simulate the pressure that may be associated with standardized test taking.
- Make certain all of the skills areas are represented, as applicable.
- Offer practice tests to gauge potential student performance on actual examinations.
- Make certain all of the question items have been vetted according to test specifications, including length (e.g. number of words,

time per sample or prompt, pause times between audio excerpts, etc.) as well as the CEFR.
• Align the content with each course's learning goals, objectives, outcomes and standards (LGOOS).

In order to create such content, teachers, curriculum developers and language programme administrators can use the assessment features of the content management platform they are using (e.g. Moodle, Blackboard, Chamilo, etc.) to create quizzes and tests. Powerful software programmes for the development of e-learning solutions are also available; in my experience, Articulate® and Adobe Captivate 9.0 have a vast variety of features that can make the content very user-friendly and highly effective. There are also free apps available for PCs and Macs, such as *EasyTestMaker*, *QuestBase* or *TestMoz*, just to name a few. To highlight their impact on learners, here are some testimonials from students at a large Latin American language centre, when asked about the value of international test familiarization resources called E-Exams, which we created (testimonials translated from Spanish):

• *'I wasn't aware of their importance at the time, but I eventually realized that the E-Exams were very helpful in getting me ready for the … test I had to take. The content was familiar to me and I had no trouble with the timing.'* – Juan
• *'The "E-Exams" helped me improve my learning of the language. Additionally, they prepared me for the international exam that came later, which I did well on by the way.'* – Maria
• *'My final result on the international test was great. I guess all of the practice in my free time paid off! The Institute did a great job in providing me with the resources I needed to do well.'* – Marco

At Euroidiomas, I have been able to maintain my philosophy of providing e-learning content and printed final exams that resemble what students will find on the world renowned Cambridge English and other examinations. While leading the institution's efforts to carry out ambitious projects with

ACTIVITY

Use an LMS, Internet-based test generator or the exam prep software that comes with the course book series you may be using, try to create an assessment that looks and feels like an international proficiency examination your students may be taking later on. Ask your students if they think it is helpful.

schools, universities, corporate clients and government agencies, I have maintained international test familiarization as a strategy for preparing students for their international examinations and an important means of validating the quality of the language study programmes we offer.

Learning Analytics and Accreditation

Learning analytics is an emerging practice within the field of English language teaching and learning. It is essentially the systematic collection of data regarding learner progress and achievement that can be used for analysis by teachers, language programme administrators, curriculum developers, materials designers, e-learning providers and international accreditation agencies. The information can be collected at level of the individual student, class section or group, branch (if there is more than one) and institutional. The technology can shed light on what aspects of the course or programmes are doing well and which ones need to improve. Table 8.3 has some examples of data types that can be collected over time.

It should be noted that international accreditation agencies require this and other types of information when they do their onsite inspections. The Evaluation and Accreditation of Quality in Language Services (EAQUALS) and the Commission on English Language Programme Accreditation (CEA) expect that information regarding learner assessment and achievement be

Table 8.3 Areas That International Accrediting Agencies May Assess

Data Type	Benefit/Ensuing Action
Pass/fail rates	If the pass or fail rates seem too high for a teacher's class or multiple groups, there may be a need to speak to the teacher and provide additional training in assessment and evaluation.
Grades per skill or knowledge area	If students in a class have a particularly low average in reading or another skill area, the teacher may decide to take corrective action. At the branch and institutional levels, there may be a need to modify and improve the curriculum for the course or instructional level.
Learner choice	If students seem to prefer a particular content, activity or task type more often than others, there may be a need to find out why in order to improve the learning experience overall.
Time of use	Determining the time students spend on accessing the content can be indicative of their levels of motivation and compliance with course requirements. If too little time is being spent, the teacher may need to discuss the matter with students to find out why, and even contemplate the possibility of changing the e-resource altogether.
Attendance/ punctuality	There may be a direct correlation between learner achievement and attendance/punctuality. The statistics may indicate that the higher performing students are attending more regularly and are tardy less often than the others who are struggling.
Achievement on international exams	The pass levels may reaffirm the perceived quality of a study programme or highlight the need to improve the curriculum in one or more areas, especially if learners are not meeting expectations.
Self-assessments	Information from periodic self-assessments may show a high degree of self-confidence and feelings of achievement, or the opposite.
Fulfilment of LGOOS/test validation	Information on learner fulfilment of course goals, objectives, outcomes and standards should be maintained. When an unusually high percentage of students do not fare well with a particular item, it may be a sign that corrective action is needed.

abundant, systematically collected and readily available and that students receive informative reporting throughout their studies. With technology-supported, standards-based assessment systems, 'educational institutions can significantly strengthen their efforts to meet accreditation requirements in the area of learner assessment' (Mercado, 2015a, p. 182).

Conclusion

In this chapter, we have touched on essential principles and concepts related to successful language assessment and how they can be applied with the support of technology. In the future, it would be ideal if data collection in the classroom by way of a smartphone or tablet could be linked to a remote server, allowing students' work and language samples to be recorded in text, audio or video formats and then sent to a repository that comes to represent their development portfolios. Pictures, voice recordings and video footage from each student could be sent to his or her portfolio simply by clicking on the right icon as class is taking place. In the meantime, we have seen the many ways in which technology can greatly facilitate learner assessment and evaluation. Most importantly, it can enhance the students' ability not only to learn the language well but also to meet international standards and benchmarks. In today's context of standards accountability, technology can make a significant contribution to language learning success.

Discussion Questions

1. What kinds of technologically supported prompts for eliciting L2 output could appeal to more than one learning style (e.g. aural, visual, kinaesthetic, etc.)?
2. How could technology help you improve your use of time when assessing speaking or writing skills in the classroom?

3. How would you get students to use an e-portfolio in order to show an improvement in their listening skills?
4. What would you use to improve your students' ability to perform well on standardized tests? What is one kind of exercise or activity you would create, and how would you do it?
5. What are some advantages of using a 'test generator' that often comes with a course book? What are some disadvantages?
6. What kinds of information do you think are the most valuable in determining your students' needs as well as identifying opportunities to improve the learning experience? How would you collect it using technology?

Suggested Readings

Burke, K. (2009). *How to Assess Authentic Learning*, 5th edn (Upper Saddle River, NJ: Merrill-Prentice Hall).
An 'oldie but a goodie' book that most opened my mind to the world of assessment.

MacDonald, R. et al. (2015) *Formative Language Assessment for English Learners: A Four-Step Process* (London: Heinemann).
Offers extensive insights on formative assessment, a practice often overlooked by teachers.

Mayrath, M. C. and J. Clarke-Midura (2012) *Technology-Based Assessments for 21st Century Skills: Theoretical and Practical Implications from Modern Research*. (Charlotte, NC: Information Age Publishing).
Addresses multiple disciplines, providing important insights on how to promote and assess creative problem solving, collaboration and technology fluency.

Mercado, L. A. (2015) Chapter 10: 'Standards-based Assessment for Young Learners', in C. N. Giannikas, L. McLoughlin and G. Fanning (eds) *Children Learning English: From Research to Practice,* Young Learners and Teenagers Special Interest Group, IATEFL (Reading: Garnett Education).
Particularly relevant for assessing all skills from a standards-based perspective.

9 Professional Development and Technology

> *Any attempt to evaluate professional development efforts for technology and instruction must carefully examine ... whether that professional development had an impact on teacher knowledge and behavior and/or specific student-learning outcomes.*
>
> Lawless and Pellegrino, 2007

We often refer to the importance of fostering learner motivation when discussing the prerequisites to successful learning experiences. However, we sometimes fail to remember that teachers are also essential protagonists of the learning process who must be equally motivated. When teacher motivation is not taken seriously, there is a risk of having teachers who may be less willing and less able to create positive, nourishing learning environments. Such a situation makes it more likely for learners to eventually lose interest and disengage from the learning process. Neves de Jesus and Lens (2005) also remind us that, 'teacher motivation is important for the satisfaction and fulfilment of teachers themselves. Beyond issues of personal well-being, such feelings of satisfaction are consistently associated with lower levels of organisational absenteeism and turnover' (p. 120). Therefore, if we are to promote successful learning, it is of utmost importance that we understand what most impacts teacher motivation and how it can be cultivated in a twenty-first-century, highly technological context. Thus, these are the questions we will consider in this chapter:

- What motivates teachers, and how can their commitment be sustained?
- What are the key alternatives teachers should prioritize for their own development, and how can technology be used in support?
- How can teachers best learn how to integrate technology throughout their students' learning experiences? What are some realizable goals?

Numerous studies indicate that teachers' motivation seems mostly affected by situational/contextual factors that can have an impact on their sense of self-efficacy, self-determination and empowerment (Dornyei and Ushioda, 2011; Hastings, 2012; Thoonen et al., 2011). Professional development is perhaps the most effective way for teachers to address their needs in all of these areas. Certainly, research has established a positive association between effective professional development and higher teacher motivation (Avalos, 2011; Latham and Vogt, 2007; Whitehurst, 2002). In terms of results, Avalos' review of 10 years' worth of studies found that, '[i]t was clear from the successful experiences narrated, that prolonged interventions are more effective than shorter ones, and that combinations of tools for learning and reflective experiences serve ... in a better way' (p. 17). Moreover, further research, literature and case studies on successful professional development programmes point to multi-tiered approaches that combine opportunities for self-learning with those that get teachers to learn from each other through cooperative development initiatives and professional learning communities, or PLCs (Edge, 2011; Lumpe, 2007; Mercado, 2013a). From a twenty-first-century perspective, professional development initiatives must also lead teachers to become proficient in the use of technology in order to better respond to the needs and expectations of their tech-savvy learners as well as make effective use of technological resources for their own learning.

Technological Proficiency and Standards

As stated in earlier chapters, teachers must be able to create learning environments that their students will embrace and appreciate. In the age of the *digital native, millennial,* and *net gener,* this means that teachers must become proficient in the use of technology. As stated earlier in this volume, many teachers are still struggling to come to terms with technology and how to make it a useful part of their everyday practice. Yet teachers should not fear technology, but rather see it as a powerful ally that will make their work easier and more effective.

In Chapter 1, I pointed out the need for teachers to develop strategies for learning enhancement through technology (SLET) and that they can achieve this in three stages. Again, there is no strict timetable to follow when it comes to developing SLET. This is because teachers are free to learn at their own pace in accordance with their particular needs and context. Another important point to remember is that no one is born a technology expert. People learn a second language and just about everything else in life from a given starting point and move on progressively until they have reached the level of mastery they wish to achieve. The same applies to technology in general and SLET in particular. What is most essential is that over time teachers develop a level of expertise in using a repertoire of technology-oriented strategies, resources and tools that will make the teaching and learning process more effective. Once mastery of SLET for general English studies has been achieved, the next professional goal can be to move on to SLET for ESP and CLIL-oriented applications, among other alternatives. In Figure 9.1, we see how teachers can transition from one stage to another as they develop SLET, learning to use a variety of tools and resources that become progressively more complex in terms of their application to the learning experience.

Looking at the broader picture, in terms of benchmarks related to specific knowledge, competencies and skills, the TESOL Technology Standards provide a useful reference for

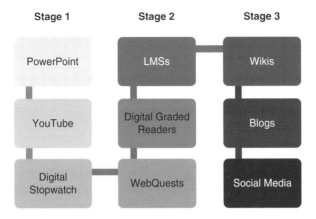

Figure 9.1 Examples of tools and resources for each stage in developing SLET.

teachers and Language Program Administrators alike. They are the result of the extensive work done by the National Educational Technology Standards (NETS) Project in the International Society for Technology in Education (ISTE), resulting in standards for language teachers and standards for language learners (TESOL, 2016). According to Healey et al. (2011), the standards lay out four overarching goals for teachers of English to meet:

1. Language teachers will develop foundational skills and knowledge in technology for professional purposes.
2. Language teachers will integrate pedagogical knowledge and skills with technology to enhance language teaching and learning.
3. Language teachers will apply technology in record-keeping, feedback and assessment.
4. Language teachers will use technology to improve communication, collaboration and efficiency as they carry out their tasks and interact with others.

These standards were created to promote teacher awareness as to the importance of using technology for language learning

ACTIVITY

Develop a plan with a timetable so you can align your teaching practice with the SLET framework and international benchmarks, such as the TESOL Technology Standards. When would you expect to be fully versed and compliant?

in more effective ways. The same applies to their own professional development. The standards for language learners, in particular, can aid teachers as they develop, implement and assess their courses and lessons, making them more amenable to the needs and expectations of the twenty-first-century learner. The standards 'are designed to be applicable to teachers and students at a range of English proficiency levels in many English language teaching and learning settings around the world' (TESOL, 2016, p. 1). Upon closer scrutiny, one could conclude that this entire volume aids teachers in meeting each and every one of these general goals along with their respective standards. Moreover, the SLET and QLL Dynamics frameworks allow teachers to become adept and confident users of technology that can maximize learning outcomes in a highly technological world while meeting international standards and benchmarks for technological literacy.

Proficiency and Background Knowledge

As mentioned in earlier chapters, many teachers of English throughout the world have a need to further develop their proficiency in the language, instructional expertise and overall knowledge of the field in order to become more effective professionals. Technology can support teachers in these key areas by facilitating the delivery of content for professional learning, promoting self-assessment and reflection, supporting teacher networks and PLCs and providing a sense of accomplishment and recognition. This will most likely help teachers maintain a high degree of commitment to their own professional development. In my experience, I have had the opportunity to create diverse programmes catering to one or all of these areas at any given time. From what I have learned, I can say that success can be ensured through efforts that have clear goals and objectives as well as a strong determination on the part of key stakeholders to bring each initiative to fruition. As another important factor, effective communication is essential in order to ensure that all stakeholders are duly informed and 'buy-in' on their part is maximized. Finally, teachers should receive extensive support that begins at the pre-service stage and continues through their crucial first year of employment until they are ultimately able to learn on their own. Within this context, the role of technology is clearly defined as a tool and resource that can enhance outcomes in teacher education and development.

With the quote at the beginning of this chapter, Lawless and Pellegrino (2007) remind us that all professional development efforts must lead to clear, discernable outcomes that reflect a positive impact on instruction and learning. This is particularly true when a programme seeks to fulfil the needs of a large number of teachers at the same time. Unfortunately, as Bailey, Curtis and Nunan (2003) point out, 'One point that is often overlooked is that teacher development must result in better teaching and learning' (p. 5) but that does not always happen. As a case study, I would like to refer to various commercially available online professional development solutions for English teachers that I had the chance to work with up close. The analysis can be summarized in Table 9.1.

This analysis leads us to two important points regarding professional development and technology: (i) the alternative should be comprehensive in nature and broad enough in scope; (ii) it should be linked to a follow-up that can confirm that what was learned can be applied. Fortunately, the offerings in the example have improved significantly over time.

Table 9.1 Analysis of a Comprehensive Online Professional Development Solution

Component	Advantage	Drawback
Language skills course with an emphasis on English for the classroom	Learning the kind of language teachers use for everyday classroom interactions and instruction, which reflects an immediate need in many EFL settings and contexts	Its usefulness is limited, and the whole approach can seem audio-lingual in nature. It cannot replace the goal of having teachers develop their overall proficiency in the language until they reach a minimum standard (e.g. B2 level according to the CEFR) and validate their knowledge and skills through a reputable international proficiency certificate.
Professional knowledge course for English teachers	Learning about the teaching and learning process through formal instruction and reflection	Without a follow-up, it is impossible to determine whether what one supposedly learned can later be applied to the classroom in the form of more effective instruction that leads to greater learning.
International Standardized Assessment	An assessment backed by a world-renowned testing agency, leading to a certificate of completion	It implies that teachers who pass the test upon completion of the course are better off than they were at the beginning. What it shows is that they 'understand' and 'know', but not that they can necessarily 'do'.

In the example, 'English for the classroom' can still be regarded as a positive first step for teachers with low levels of language proficiency (i.e. A1 or A2 level according to the CEFR) who are already working in ELT institutions, particularly outside of the 'inner-circle' countries. Nevertheless, in the quest for effective professional development solutions, teachers should also simultaneously engage in mid- to long-term solutions that will allow them to fully develop their language proficiency until they reach a minimum standard, thus attaining the degree of confidence and professional competence they may feel they sorely need. Such a standard has been cited to be an A2 or B1 level of English according to the CEFR for primary level instruction and a B2 level or its equivalent for secondary school and higher (Baldauf et al., 2013; Cardenas, 2006; Cely, 2015; Chambless, 2012; Government of Chile, 2014). Let us not forget that the job entrusted to English teachers is to help learners develop their proficiency in the language over time. Students must go from elementary levels of communication to the more fully developed grammatical, sociolinguistic, discourse and strategic competences that are needed to perform successfully in a broad range of contexts, most of which are likely to be of a highly diverse and challenging nature (Canale and Swain, 1980; O'Maggio-Hadley, 2001). Along the way, the teacher serves as a fundamental source of L2 input and is thus often called upon to expand on the limited examples of language found in course books and supplementary materials. Metaphorically speaking, a teacher's mind may be seen by learners as a 'language repository' of sorts that can serve as an important source of 'real-world' and 'real-life' examples of English, which can be explained and clarified upon request. Therefore, the higher the teachers' level of proficiency in English and the more life experiences they may have in its use, the more likely it is that they will be able to fulfil their students' needs and expectations for such a perceived role. Of course, as Harmer (2007) reminds us, 'When we are acting as resource, we will want to be helpful and available, but at the same time

ACTIVITY

Think about an aspect of your language proficiency or background knowledge in SLA/methodology that you would like to improve. Review at least three professional development alternatives that could help you. What criteria for selection would you employ?

we have to resist the urge to spoonfeed our students so that they become over-reliant on us' (p. 110).

Regarding the issue of following up on virtual learning experiences, I have already stated in previous chapters that learners must eventually be called upon to demonstrate to the classroom their ability to apply to what they have learned on their own and eventually in the 'real-world', especially if the learning cycle is to be considered successful. In the case of teachers, simply passing what may very well be a well-designed online assessment may not be sufficient unless the result can be further substantiated by classroom observations, video recordings, student surveys, focus groups and other data sources that can confirm that instruction and learning have both improved. Only then can we bring closure to such a professional development cycle.

Professional Development Programmes for Teachers

We must deal with a reality that many become English teachers after first exploring other career tracks and that they may not necessarily meet the minimum standards for language proficiency often cited in the field (Mercado, 2013a). Furthermore, some studies show that teachers may feel there is a significant gap between their current level of proficiency in the language and what they feel is appropriate for their students, having a possible detrimental effect on their performance, motivation and overall sense of achievement (Butler, 2004; Eslami and Fatahi, 2008). Therefore, obtaining credentials that can validate their proficiency in the language can have a highly motivating effect, providing both a sense of direction in their professional development and a sense of accomplishment that can counteract problems related to self-efficacy and self-esteem. Moreover, Ministries of Education throughout the world have set proficiency targets for teachers as part of large-scale, national projects whose purpose is to raise the quality of English language learning in their public school systems. Table 9.2 shows examples of programmes I designed for a Ministry of Education in South America.

Table 9.2 Overview of Tailor-made Blended & 100% Online Learning Programmes for Teachers

Target Group	Length of Programme	Target CEFR Levels (as Specified by the Ministry of Education)	Technology
Secondary School teachers of English (2010–2011)	6 months, 200-hour courses, 2-year programme	A2, B1 & B2, with international certificates. Ultimate goal: B2.	Online platform for 40% of the study hours (minimum 80 hours out of 200 for each course), blended
Secondary School teachers of English (2016–2017)	12 months, up to 840 hours 8 months, 400 hours	B1 & B2, with international certificates Main goal: B1 Ultimate goal: B2	Online platform for 100% of the study hours/ Ongoing video-conferencing

As discussed in Chapter 3, the programme for teachers in 2010–11 was an enormous success because practically all of the close to 4000 teachers participating nationwide met or exceeded their proficiency targets, as exemplified by their results on the international proficiency examinations they took; there was low desertion or turnover, and the teachers exhibited exceptionally high satisfaction rates. The programme included a robust, commercially sold platform for the online content, a standardized curriculum, a methodological approach with differentiated instructional strategies, and rigorous training for the instructors. Similar results are expected for the new 2016–2017 programme following the same approach. However, rather than wait for a government-funded programme, teachers may want to develop their proficiency in the language on their own. There are numerous face-to-face, blended and 100 per cent virtual solution alternatives, many of which have already been discussed in previous chapters of this volume. In order to choose the best alternatives among blended or 100 per cent online programmes, teachers should keep the following in mind:

- Any LMS, MOOC or other technological learning resource that is meant to promote language learning should be robust, providing enough hours of exposure to the language and opportunities for learning and practice (extensive content).
- The level of English and diversity of language skills required from teachers is often greater than it is for learners. This is important to remember for goal-setting purposes.
- It is essential to set goals and objectives within a time frame (e.g. 'obtain a Cambridge English KET certificate by … '; 'I need a 90 on the TOEFL iBT, so I must study for…').
- Discipline is required in terms of the amount of effort that must be made, compliance with course goals and assessments, and time management so that the learning process is ongoing and uninterrupted.

As for professional knowledge of SLA theory and what I call generally accepted teaching and learning principles (GATLP), there are a variety of technologically supported, commercial options available on the market. When working with commercial products that are aimed at professional development and training for teachers, it would probably be best if they offered the following (Figure 9.2):

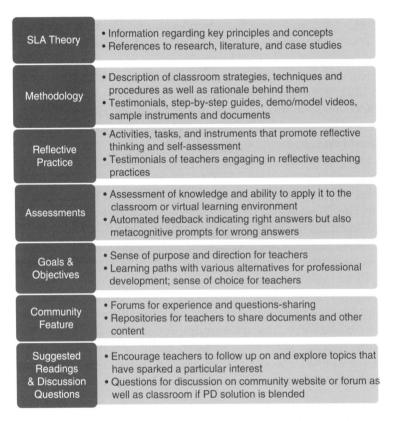

SLA Theory	• Information regarding key principles and concepts • References to research, literature, and case studies
Methodology	• Description of classroom strategies, techniques and procedures as well as rationale behind them • Testimonials, step-by-step guides, demo/model videos, sample instruments and documents
Reflective Practice	• Activities, tasks, and instruments that promote reflective thinking and self-assessment • Testimonials of teachers engaging in reflective teaching practices
Assessments	• Assessment of knowledge and ability to apply it to the classroom or virtual learning environment • Automated feedback indicating right answers but also metacognitive prompts for wrong answers
Goals & Objectives	• Sense of purpose and direction for teachers • Learning paths with various alternatives for professional development; sense of choice for teachers
Community Feature	• Forums for experience and questions-sharing • Repositories for teachers to share documents and other content
Suggested Readings & Discussion Questions	• Encourage teachers to follow up on and explore topics that have sparked a particular interest • Questions for discussion on community website or forum as well as classroom if PD solution is blended

Figure 9.2 Fundamental areas for online PD solutions for teachers.

The above 'checklist' can be used by teachers and LPAs alike. What could probably magnify the positive effects of online professional development programmes is human intervention. Online mentors and tutors should be available throughout each course as teachers come to terms with the rigors of understanding the content, assessments, etc. As with students, teachers may be less likely to take an online course seriously and allot the time it requires if no one is around to monitor their work and progress. Extensive research and literature on professional development for teachers favour the inclusion of ongoing support and opportunities for teachers to talk to each other about the work they do each and every day (Wilson and Berne, 1999). Therefore, virtual professional development programmes that promote interaction among "students" and their instructors are perhaps more likely to succeed than those alternatives which are entirely self-directed. In addition, research has shown that ongoing support, along with professional development opportunities, can further reduce the possibility of teacher burnout and the decision on their part to leave the field (Ingersoll, 2001). Apart from commercial alternatives, they can also be 'home-made' with a little creativity and much work.

Based on my previous experiences, I have had teachers use different alternatives, depending on their stage of professional development in the field. In one case, it took me 10 years to build a solid, comprehensive professional development programme. Now that I am currently 'starting all-over again' at my new institution, I have gone back to setting the first building blocks of a new programme for teacher education and development. Table 9.3 illustrates some of the alternatives I have applied successfully at different times throughout my career as well as the roles technology has been assigned.

In the case of online course series guides and publisher-developed teacher training websites, the more teachers understand the underlying philosophy and purpose of their teaching materials, the better use they will make of them. During a large-scale course series change, for example, I asked a publisher to create such a website because I knew: (i) we were hiring new teachers on a permanent basis and that coming to understand the new course book series was an important

Table 9.3 Professional Development Alternatives Supported by Technology

Stage in Career and Professional Development	Technological Professional Development Alternative	Benefits
Pre- or In-service	Online course series guide/teacher training websites (publishers or 'home-made')	Teachers become familiar with the course book, scope and sequence, learning goals and objectives, content, and suggested instructional approach (i.e. classes videos).
Pre- or In-service	Peer observation	Teachers can learn from colleagues and language programme administrators by watching one another's video recordings of their classes.
In-service	E-portfolios	Teachers can develop digital compilations of their work through various stages of their development.
In-service	Self-observation	Teachers can learn from themselves by audio or video recording their classes, either segments or entire sessions.
In-service	Journal Writing/ Recording	Teachers can record their thoughts and insights immediately after a class session and engage in reflection for self-assessment and self-awareness.
In-service	Action Research	Teachers can engage in exploratory practice or full-blown action research, using technology to prompt learners to produce language samples, participate, use metacognition, etc.; it can also be used to record, analyse and retrieve data upon need.

aspect of their pre-service training; (ii) the more our current faculty understood the new series and the more tools were available to make its implementation a success, the better chances there were that the overall transformational change process would also succeed.

Based on our requirements, the publisher created a website that included a description of all of the activity types as well as examples of from the different levels of the book, discussion and reflection questions for the teacher to answer after learning about each component of the series and its contents, samples of course book pages, and videos of demo classes to show a teacher who is new to the series how to put the book to good use. From what I have seen over the years, this last feature is particularly important for novice and experienced teachers alike since they always seem to need a model to which they can refer. It also takes the resource beyond the role of simply delivering expository content by bringing the course book series to life through the depiction on video of real classes with real students. When such a website is lacking, an institution's language programme administrators (e.g. supervisors, curriculum developers, etc.) can create one from scratch using a variety of software, apps and other tools, including the following:

- Microsoft PowerPoint, Prezi and commercially available software, such as Articulate, Adobe Presenter and Adobe Captivate, which convert presentations into e-learning courses and offer a wide variety of other powerful features.
- Blogs, YouTube and 'homemade' videos.
- Wix.com, Weebly.com and other free website-creation apps.
- Clouds to store and share digital media (e.g. videos, documents, etc.).

Reflection and Technology

In Chapter 8, we discussed the use of e-portfolios for language learners as means to collect samples of student performance and progress. Teachers can also collect samples of their work and benefit from the kind of prolonged interventions and reflective practices that Avalos (2011) and other researchers have found to be so effective. Certainly, the tendency to move to teacher portfolios has been on the rise. Analysing the use of portfolios in the United States, Hallman (2007) recently found that 'that among the 89% of schools or colleges of education that use some type of portfolio system for assessment of beginning teachers ... many are moving from hard-copy portfolio form to electronic form' (p. 475). In terms of what should be included, teachers should always be given a choice because it is supposed to be a very personal compilation of their work and thinking that substantiates their progression from one stage of development to another. Bailey, Curtis and Nunan (2003), however, warn LPAs and institutions from presenting teachers 'with a shopping list of items they are expected to compile, often in an insufficient period of time' (p. 227). Needless to say, such a practice would distort the very purpose and nature of a teaching portfolio. We should always keep in mind that a teaching portfolio is what Farrell (2015) calls 'an evolving collection of carefully selected professional experiences, thoughts, and goals [that] can be accompanied with the teacher's written (or oral) reflection and self-assessment of the collection itself and plans for the future' (p. 24). He goes on further to state that a teaching portfolio can include a teaching philosophy, a description of teaching goals and responsibilities, materials that the teacher has created and

ACTIVITY

Create a teaching portfolio account with an app such as *Pathbrite*. Identify four main areas for which you would like to document your growth and achievement as an ELT professional and begin to collect your artifacts and other information. Whom would you like to share your portfolio with eventually?

evidence of teacher performance and effectiveness from learner and peer feedback.

Now it is time we discuss one of the most powerful professional development alternatives of them all: PLCs. Without a supportive, community-oriented working environment, teachers can feel isolated and even lonely. This brings out the need to create opportunities for teachers to interact with colleagues in order to find support and a sense of belonging. This is why coordinators/LPAs should introduce PLCs as soon as possible (Diaz-Maggioli, 2004; Vescio, Ross and Adams, 2008) in order to:

- foster mutually supportive reflection on teachers' day-to-day work;
- lead to empathetic support when problems arise;
- promote sharing of best practices as well as a plethora of other ideas on how to improve instructional efficacy; and
- create a simple, yet all-important sense of belonging.

In their review of 10 studies in the United States and one in the United Kingdom, Vescio, Ross and Adams (2008), for example, found that PLCs can have a positive impact on teaching practice and student achievement. From a technological perspective, PLCs can be supported by blogs, wikis, online forums/communities, audio and video recording features on tablets and smartphones, clouds for data and media storage, PowerPoint/Prezi for teacher conferences and so on.

One professional development alternative that can serve as support for a PLC is peer observation. Technologically speaking, the sharing of videos is a convenient practice that supersedes the time and scheduling limitations often associated with class observations that are in done in person. Needless to say, the virtues and benefits of peer observation are well known, not only in our field but in education as a whole. As Bailey, Curtis and Nunan (2003) point out, peer observation can serve to break down barriers between teachers within a professional learning community (PLC) and promote fruitful, reflective academic discussion. A study conducted by Hammersly-Fletcher and Orsmond (2004) at the higher

education level found that teachers who engage in peer observation can centre their reflective focus on their teaching practices and the use of teaching materials, but that opportunities
should not be lost for teachers to discuss what reflection is and
how it can be used for maximum effect. In addition, the study
highlighted the fact that effective relationships are crucial for
peer observation to succeed, fostering non-judgemental, constructive feedback and 'honest reflection within a process
where confidentiality is assured' (p. 217). The purpose should
always be clear, so, as Richards and Lockhart (1997) explain,
'Peer observation should be approached as an opportunity for
teachers to help each other collect information that would
be useful to them and which they could not obtain on their
own…. Teachers should see themselves as co-researchers collaborating for each others' [sic] benefit' (p. 5).

In practice, peer observation only requires a digital recorder
and a tripod, a tablet or even a smartphone. Of course, the
larger and more powerful the device, the wider the view of the
class, the better the recording of the audio and video, and
the more footage that can be recorded. Nevertheless, the scope of
the coverage in class will depend on the focus of the observation,
which should be agreed between the observed and the observer
prior to the viewing of the video. Videos recorded on a tablet or
smartphone can be uploaded to a cloud, such as Google Drive,
iCloud, or Dropbox, just to name some examples. Then they can
be shared among teachers.

There are also apps that can guide in-person peer observations, such as *iAspire, Classroom Monitor, Classroom Observation,
iObserve* and others, some of which are free and others that
come with a cost. They all basically organize data that one
can collect during a class observation. The advantage with
such apps is that they allow the observer to click on the assessment criteria values that most represent what they are watching, without having to take down notes. They also allow for
audio and video recording of lesson segments that can be 'time
stamped' to indicate where the teacher met the criteria or

where they may have been a critical incident. Needless to say, such recordings make the observations less judgemental and more objective.

Another important option is self-observation as it allows teachers to see themselves and then assess their teaching according their own expectations and standards. In a survey that I administered to 247 teachers, the following responses were cited as among the most important when it came to perceived benefits from self-observation:

- Helps one see one's strengths and opportunities for improvement: 87.5 per cent.
- Creates opportunities for reflection: 80.2 per cent.
- Aids in making instructional decisions: 65.6 per cent.
- Creates opportunities to observe student behaviour: 57.1 per cent (Mercado and Baecher, 2014).

Continuing with cooperative learning opportunities, technology can do much in the way of audio and video recordings and reflections. In a study by Dettori and Luppi (2013), L2 learners of French were asked to use a software programme for audio editing, called Audacity, to record their voice samples as they practised with model pronunciation exercises online. The methodology involved having the learners do a number of tasks that increased in difficulty progressively, with students recording their samples individually. Then, as a group, they reviewed their recordings one by one, analysing each sample,

ACTIVITY

During a lesson, activate your voice recorder on your smartphone or tablet. Leave it on for five minutes, and listen to it after class. Who is doing most of the talking? If you are, how could you change your approach so that your students are heard more often?

using metacognitive language as trained by the teacher and correcting the samples through collaborative feedback. Each recording was reviewed by the group of three students and re-recorded individually until it was deemed satisfactory and ready for final submission. The researchers found the use of the software preferable to voice recorders and other devices because it allowed for editing and improved quality in the recordings. In terms of time frames and kinds of exercises, Dettori and Lupi explain that:

> [a]ctivities of this kind are repeated several times over a few months, with increasingly complex recordings, until pronunciation confidence and a satisfactory level of proficiency are reached. Each student collects all her/his recordings in a sort of audio portfolio witnessing her/his improvement. (p. 621)

Needless to say, the methodology employed in this study can be easily applied to teachers, and the collection of recordings as a way to create an e-portfolio ties in with what we have been discussing throughout this chapter. There are three lessons from this study, supported by extensive research, that apply to teacher professional development: (i) collaborative review and metacognition can improve results in language training and language production; (ii) recycling tasks and increasing the level of difficulty progressively can lead to better results; and (iii) collecting samples of work through e-portfolios is likely to make teachers more cognizant of their progress and achievements.

ACTIVITY

Create a list of five questions you would like to ask your peers. Which one is the most important for you? How can you 'get it out there' and resolve your doubts?

Finally, PLCs can be supported enormously if teachers have a venue through which they can pose questions, exchange ideas, share experiences and demonstrate what they know how to do well. One alternative is to have a teacher conference, either face-to-face or virtual, in which teachers can present their ideas and experiences through academic sessions. If it is face-to-face, teachers can use Microsoft PowerPoint or Prezi to present their ideas; demonstrations and exhibits with YouTube videos and apps or software can make a session more engaging, meaningful and comprehensible to their colleagues in the audience. Another alternative is to have an online forum through a learning management platform (e.g. Moodle, Blackboard, or Chamilo) or one afforded by the numerous free websites that are available to teachers, LPAs and institutions alike. Teachers can interact with their peers to discuss common teaching and other issues, sharing ideas and experiences. When such a platform is not available, a blog can be created by the coordinator or – even better – the teachers themselves. When possible and appropriate, a coordinator should be assigned as a moderator and should post at least one discussion question or elicit a topic to focus on each week, while teachers should be encouraged to participate as much as possible.

Conclusion

This chapter linked technology to professional development for teachers. From SLET and online courses to tools for self-assessment and PLCs, teachers can enrich their professional development and teacher-training experiences enormously with the support of technology. Positive results should be associated with every effort, with teachers determining their own learning paths and timetables according to their needs and expectations. The ultimate goal is for teachers to come to embrace technology as a friend and ally that can accompany them throughout their careers. Once they have developed a high level of proficiency in SLET, they will be in a better position to adapt to the ever faster changes that we can expect to be brought on from the technologies of the future.

Discussion Questions

1. How would you adapt your everyday lesson planning and teaching practice to SLET and international benchmarks such as the TESOL Technology Standards?
2. Have you ever had a negative experience involving professional development? Could technology have changed the outcome?
3. What is it about blended learning solutions for learning English that can make them so successful? Would a blended learning solution work for you? How about 100 per cent online?
4. Are teacher training demo videos important in your opinion? Would you find them helpful? Would you share your own? Why or why not?
5. Why do you think an e-portfolio can be so helpful for teachers? What would you include in yours? Why?
6. Would you present at a teacher conference at your school, university or language centre? Why or why not? If so, what would you present, and how could technology make your presentation more effective?

Suggested Readings

Edge, J. and S. Mann (2013) *Innovations in Pre-service Education and Training for English Language Teachers* (Manchester: British Council).
Presents 14 papers regarding professional development opportunities for pre-service and novice teachers alike, including technological alternatives.

Mercado, L. A. (2012) *English Language Learning and Technology* (Boston, MA: Cengage Learning).

Includes a chapter (8) on standards for teachers in an age of technology, including ideas on professional development and language proficiency development.

Nunan, D. and J. C. Richards. (2015) *Language Learning beyond the Classroom* (New York: Routledge).

Presents 28 different papers on autonomous learning, many of which rely heavily on technology for successful implementation, making the volume an important source of insights on how teachers can improve their SLET over time.

Glossary

benchmarks Expectations, objectives or standards for achievement and success that are associated with a referential model.

CBI/CBL Content-based instruction and content-based learning. Similar to CLIL in that language learning takes place as learners use the second language to learn about diverse topics and subject areas.

classroom and autonomous learning integration (CALI) The systematic and purposeful integration of classroom learning and autonomous learning processes.

CLIL Content and language integrated learning. Learners develop their language skills while focusing their learning on a major subject area, such as maths, geography and so on.

context A current, desired or anticipated situation or state that serves as a frame of reference for language use in any of its forms (e.g. words, phrases, sentences, etc.).

curriculum teaching Teaching method in which teachers concentrate on developing in their students the content knowledge or cognitive skills that are represented on a test.

curricular vetting A process by which contents (e.g. L2 input, exercises, activities, audios, videos, etc.) are reviewed, evaluated and primed for inclusion in a curriculum.

digital natives Those born into a world of technology and for whom technology is a natural part of their everyday lives.

enriched input/input flood A more implicit approach that presents learners with input that contains a high number of exemplars of the target form or forms without any overt marking or references in order to help them notice the language features on their own.

extensive reading Reading that is for the purpose of enjoyment or leisure at the reader or learner's discretion.

flipped learning A modality of learning that has instructional input (i.e. lectures, podcasts, videos, etc.) delivered for learners to access on their own so that time in the classroom is dedicated to activities and tasks for meaningful practice, problem-solving and the development of higher-order thinking skills.

form-focused instruction Any type of instruction that addresses form in an explicit or implicit manner and is either planned or incidental in nature.

HTML-5 A programming code that is now considered the standard for making applications, and content in general, mobile compatible ('responsive' so that it displays well on any device).

intensive reading Reading and reading skills development that take place within an instructional setting under the guidance of a teacher.

interactive white board (IWB) A digital whiteboard that facilitates the delivery, highlighting and modification of content for the whole class to see.

interactive writing strategy Method in which students write freely without regard for structure or organization so they may identify main ideas on a topic, and then construct a whole new text from the main ideas identified in the previous stage without referring to the original sample.

interlanguage The language system that learners use and exhibit at any given time as they seek to achieve proficiency.

international test familiarization Having learners practice with contents that will help them gain knowledge of the kinds of questions, instructions, time constraints and overall formatting considerations that they will encounter on an international proficiency test, without 'teaching to the test'.

interproficiency The current or transitory level of a learner's proficiency, as defined by international standards and benchmarks, at any time during the learning process (e.g. A2–, B2+, C1, weak B1, etc.) as learners seek to achieve a target or end level.

item teaching Teaching method in which most of the instruction is dedicated to actual or 'look-alike' items that are likely to be found on a standardized test.

learning analytics The systematic collection of data regarding learner progress and achievement that can be used for analysis and follow-up.

LGOOS Learning goals, objectives, outcomes and standards.

MALL Mobile-assisted language learning.

millennials Those who were born roughly around the year 1980 or after and who became adults at the turn of the century. They have certain characteristics that distinguish them from other generations, including a significant preference for using technology.

MOOC A massive open online course that is free and provides unlimited access for any subject area.

PBL Project-based learning, which involves having individual students or groups work on one or more tasks over a period of time, usually outside of the classroom setting.

process instruction (PI) A process that involves exposure to input, input processing, accommodation and restructuring of the interlanguage, and eventually output.

situated learning Learning that takes place in a real-life setting rather than in a classroom.

SLET Strategies for learning enhancement through technology.

structured input Content that specifically focuses the learner's attention on a target form or target forms, often relying on textual enhancement (e.g. highlighting, boldfacing, underlining and other measures).

technology Digital or electronically based devices, resources or processes that facilitate the teacher and learners' ability to think, perform, and succeed.

References

Acurio, L. (2015) Minedu capacitará a 11 mil docentes de inglés en el uso de modernas herramientas de enseñanza. Ministry of Education of Peru (accessed 15 February 2016 from http://www.minedu.gob.pe/noticias/index.php?id=34431).

Anderson, N. J. (2008) *Practical English Language Teaching: Reading* (New York: McGraw Hill.)

Anderson, L. W., D. R. Krathwohl, P. W. Airasian, K. A. Cruikshank, R. E. Mayer, P. R. Pintrich, J. Raths and M. C. Wittrock (2001) *A Taxonomy for Learning, Teaching, and assessing: A Revision of Bloom's Taxonomy of Educational Objectives* (New York: Pearson, Allyn and Bacon).

Arevart, S. and P. Nation (1991) 'Fluency Improvement in a Second Language', *RELC Journal,* 22(1), pp. 84–94.

Arnold, N. (2008) 'Online Extensive Reading for Advanced Foreign Language Learners: An Evaluation Study', *Foreign Language Annals*, 42(2), pp. 340–66.

Avalos, B. (2011) 'Teacher Professional Development in Teaching and Teacher Education over Ten Years,' *Teaching and Teacher Education*, 27, pp. 10–20.

Bailey, K. (2003) Chapter 3: 'Speaking', in D. Nunan (ed.) *Practical English Language Teaching* (New York: McGraw Hill) pp.47–66.

Bailey, K. M. (2005) *Practical English Language Teaching: Speaking* (New York: McGraw-Hill).

Bailey, K. M., A. Curtis and D. Nunan (2003) *Pursuing Professional Development: The Self as Source* (Boston, MA: Heinle & Heinle, Thomson Learning).

Bandura, A. (1977) 'Self-Efficacy: Toward a Unifying Theory of Behavioral Change', *Psychological Review,* 84(2), pp. 191–215.

Baldauf, R. B., R. B. Kaplan, K. Kamwangamalu and P. Bryant (2013) *Language Planning in Primary Schools in Asia* (London and New York: Routledge).

Beatty, K. (2013) 'Beyond the Classroom: Mobile Learning the Wider World', The International Research Foundation for English Language Education (accessed 26 September 2015 from http://www.tirfonline.org/wp-content/uploads/2013/12/TIRF_MALL_Papers_Beatty.pdf).

Barrett, H. C. (2007) 'Researching Electronic Portfolios and Learner Engagement: The REFLECT Initiative', *Journal of Adolescent and Adult Literacy*, 50(6), pp. 436–49.

Beckett, G. H. (2006) 'Project-based Second and Foreign Language Education: Theory, Research and Practice', in G. H. Beckett and P. Chamness Miller (eds) *Project-based Second and Foreign Language Education: Past, Present and Future* (Greenwich, CT: Information Age).

Bell, S. (2010) 'Project-based Learning for the 21st Century: Skills for the Future', *The Clearing House*, 83, pp. 39–43.

Bennett, S. (2012) 'Digital Natives', in Z. Yan (ed.) *Encyclopedia of Cyber Behavior*, vol. 1 (United States: IGI Global).

Berrett, D. (2012) 'How "Flipping" the Classroom Can Improve the Traditional Lecture', *The Chronicle of Higher Education*, pp. 1–14 (accessed 15 May 2015 from https://moodle.technion.ac.il/file.php/1298/Announce/How_Flipping_the_Classroom_Can_Improve_the_Traditional_Lecture.pdf).

Bishop, J. W. and M. A. Verleger (2013) 'The Flipped Classroom: A Survey of the Research', 120th ASEE Annual Conference & Exposition, 23–26 June, paper ID #6219 (accessed 15 May 2015 from https://www.asee.org/public/conferences/20/papers/6219/view).

Bitner, N. and J. Bitner (2002) 'Integrating Technology into the Classroom: Eight Keys to Success', *Journal of Technology and Teacher Education*, 10(1), pp. 95–100.

Blake, R. (2008) 'Distance Learning for Second and Foreign Language Teaching', in N. Deusen-Scholl and N. H. Hornberger (eds) *Second and Foreign Language Education: Encyclopedia of Language and Education*, vol. 4 (New York: Springer), pp. 365–76.

Brabeck, M., J. Jeffrey and S. Fry (2015) 'Practice for Knowledge Acquisition (Not Drill and Kill)', *American Psychological Association* (accessed 15 June 2015 from http://www.apa.org/education/k12/practice-acquisition.aspx).

Briggs, S. (2013) '10 Emerging Educational Technologies and How They Are Being Used around the Globe', Innovation Excellence (accessed 12 May 2015 from http://www.innovationexcellence. com/blog/2013/07/29/10-emerging-educational-technologies-how-they-are-being-used-across-the-globe/).

Brookhart, S. M. (1997) 'Classroom Assessment: Pervasive, Pivotal, and Primary', *National Forum*, 77(4), p. 3 (accessed 31 December 2015 from Questia Research Database).

Brown, H. D. (2007) *Principles of Language Learning and Teaching*, 5th edn (New York: Pearson Education).

Browne, C., B. Culligan and J. Phillips (2013) 'A New General Service List (1.01): The Most Important Words for Second Language Learners of English (accessed 15 May 2016 from http://www.newgeneralservicelist.org).

Butler, Y. G. (2004) 'What Level of English Proficiency Do Elementary School Teachers Need to Attain to Teach EFL? Case Studies from Korea, Taiwan, and Japan', *TESOL Quarterly*, 38(2), pp. 245–78.

Canale, M. and M. Swain (1980) 'Theoretical Bases of Communicative Approaches to Second Language Teaching and Testing', *Applied Linguistics*, 1, pp. 1–4.

Cardenas, M. L. (2006) 'Bilingual Colombia: Are We Ready for It? What Is Needed?', presented at the 19th Annual EA Education Conference 2006, Perth, Australia.

Celce-Murcia, M. and E. Olshtain (2000) *Discourse and Context in Language Teaching: A Guide for Language Teachers* (Cambridge, UK: Cambridge University Press).

Cely, R. M. (2015) Participation as representative of the Colombian Ministry of Education at the International Summit for Policies on English Teaching and Learning, the Peruvian Ministry of Education Convention Centre, November 30.

Chalhoub-Deville, M. (2001) 'Language Testing and Technology: Past and Future', *Language Learning and Technology*, 5(2), pp. 95–98.

Chambless, K. S. (2012) 'Teachers' Oral Proficiency in the Target Language: Research on Its Role in Language Teaching and Learning', *Foreign Language Annals*, 45(1), pp. 141–62.

Cheng, L. and A. Curtis (2004) Chapter 1: 'Washback or Backwash: A Review of the Impact of Testing on Teaching and Learning', in L. Cheng, Y. Watanabe and A. Curtis (eds) *Washback in Language Testing: Research Methods and Contexts* (Mahwah, NJ: Lawrence Erlbaum Associates), pp. 3–18.

Christison, M. A. and K. J. Krahnke (1986) 'Student Perceptions of Academic Language Study', *TESOL Quarterly*, 20(1), pp. 60–80.

Collentine, J. (2004) Chapter 8: 'Commentary: Where PI Research Has Been and Where It Should Be Going', in B. Van Patten (ed.) *Processing Instruction: Theory, Research, and Commentary* (Mahwah, NJ: Lawrence Erlbaum), pp. 169–82.

Color ABC (2009) 'MEC prefiere "pizarras interactivas", pese a que en México fue un fracaso', 2 August (accessed from http://www.abc.com.py/edicion-impresa/locales/mec-prefiere-pizarras-interactivas-pese-a-que-en-mexico-fue-un-fracaso-7490.html).

Council of Europe (2001) *Common European Framework of Reference for Languages* (Cambridge, UK: Cambridge University Press).

Crystal, D. (2008) 'Two Thousand Million?', *English Today*, 24(8), pp. 3–6.

Csikszentmihalyi, M. (2014) *Flow and the Foundations of Positive Psychology: The Collected Works of Mihaly Csikszentmihalyi* (New York: Springer).

Dafei, D. (2007) 'An Exploration of the Relationship between Learner Autonomy and English Proficiency', *Professional Teaching Article*, 1–23.

Dale, P. (2012) 'Teaching Pronunciation Successfully', presentation at the Teacher Development Conference, ICPNA, 27 February, Lima, Peru.

Davies, A. and P. Le Mahieu (2003) 'Assessment for Learning: Reconsidering Portfolios and Research Evidence', in M. Segers, F. Dochy and E. Cascallar (eds) *Innovation and Change in Professional Education: Optimising New Modes of Assessment: In Search of Qualities and Standards* (Dordrecht: Kluwer Academic Publishers), p. 141–69.

Deci, E. L., R. J. Vallerand, L. G. Pelletier and R. M. Ryan (1991) 'Motivation and Education: The Self-Determination Perspective', *Educational Pyschologist*, 26(3&4), pp. 325–46.

Desveaux, S. (2015) 'Guided Learning Hours', Cambridge English Language Assessment Support Site (accessed 15 May 2015 from https://support.cambridgeenglish.org/hc/en-gb/articles/202838506-Guided-learning-hours).

Dettori, G. and V. Luppi (2013) Chapter 40: 'Self-Observation and Shared Reflection to Improve Pronunciation in L2', in R. Azevedo and V. Aleven (eds) *International Handbook of Metacognition and Learning Technologies*, Springer International Handbooks of

Education, vol. 28 (New York: Springer Science+Business Media), pp. 615–25.

Diaz-Maggioli, G. (2004) *Teacher-Centred Professional Development* (Alexandria, VA: ASCD).

Dickinson, L. (1995) 'Autonomy and Motivation: A Literature Review', *System*, 23(2), pp. 165–74.

Dincer, A., S. Yesilyurt, and M. Takkac (2012) 'The Effects of Autonomy-Supportive Climates on EFL Learner's Engagement, Achievement and Competence in English Speaking Classrooms', *Procedia – Social and Behavioral Sciences*, 46, pp. 3890–94.

Dörnyei, Z. (1994) 'Motivation and Motivating in the Foreign Language Classroom', *The Modern Language Journal*, 78(3), pp. 273–84.

Dörnyei, Z. and E. Ushioda (2009) Chapter 1: 'Motivation, Language Identities, and the L2 Self: A Theoretical Overview', in Z. Dörnyei and E. Ushioda (eds), *Motivation, Language Identity, and the L2 Self* (Bristol: Multilingual Matters).

Dörnyei, Z. and Ushioda, E. (2011) Chapter 24: 'Motivation', in S. M. Gass and A. Mackey (eds) *The Routledge Handbook of Second Language Acquisition* (London and New York: Routledge), pp. 396–409.

Douglas, D. and L. Selinker (1985) 'Principles for Language Tests within the 'Discourse Domains' Theory of Interlanguage: Research, Test Construction and Interpretation', *Language Testing*, 2(2), pp. 205–26.

Edge, J. (2011) *The Reflexive Teacher Educator in TESOL* (London and New York: Routledge).

Ellis, R. (1999) *Second Language through Interaction* (Amsterdam: John Benjamins B.V.).

Ellis, R. (2001) 'Introduction: Investigating Form-Focused Instruction', *Language Learning*, 51(s1), pp. 1–46.

Ellis, R. (2002) 'Does Form-Focused Instruction Affect the Acquisition of Implicit Knowledge? A Review of the Research', *Studies in Second Language Acquisition*, 24(2), pp. 223–36.

Ellis, R. (2005) *Instructed Second Language Acquisition: A Literature Review: Report to the Ministry of Education* (Auckland, New Zealand: Auckland UniServices).

Ellis, R. (2006) 'Current Issues in the Teaching of Grammar: An SLA Perspective', *TESOL Quarterly*, 40(1), pp. 83–107.

Engh, D. (2013) 'Why Use Music in English Language Learning? A Survey of the Literature', *English Language Teaching*, 6(2), pp.113–27.

Ertmer, P. A., A. T. Ottenbreit-Leftwich, O. Sadik, E. Senderur and P. Senderur (2012) 'Teacher Beliefs and Technology Integration Practices: A Critical Relationship', *Computers & Education*, 59, pp. 423–35.

Eslami, Z. R. and A. Fatahi (2008) 'Teachers' Sense of Self-Efficacy, English Proficiency, and Instructional Strategies: A Study of Nonnative EFL teachers in Iran', *Teaching English as a Second Language – Electronic Journal (TESL-EJ)*, 11(4) (accessed 14 January 2016 from http://www.tesl-ej.org/wordpress/issues/volume11/ej44/ej44a1/).

Extensive Reading Foundation (n.d.) 'What Are Graded Readers?' (accessed 15 December 2015 from http://erfoundation.org/wordpress/graded-readers/).

Extensive Reading Foundation (2011) The Extensive Reading Foundation's Guide to Extensive Reading (accessed from: http://erfoundation.org/ERF_Guide.pdf).

Farrell, T. S. C. (2015) *Reflective Language Teaching: From Research to Practice* (Bloomsbury: Continuum).

Finch, A. (2001) 'Autonomy: Where Are We? Where Are We Going?', presentation at the JALT CUE Conference on Autonomy (accessed from http://www.finchpark.com/arts/Autonomy.pdf).

Fitzpatrick, A. and R. O'Dowd (2012) 'English at Work: An Analysis of Case Reports about English Language Training for the 21st-century Workforce', The International Research Foundation for English Language Education – TIRF (accessed 1 March 2016 from http://www.tirfonline.org/english-in-the-workforce/).

Froschauer, L. and M. L. Bigelow (2012) *Rise and Shine: A Practical Guide for the Beginning Science Teacher* (Arlington, VA: NSTA Press).

Galbraith, D. and M. Torrance (2004) 'Revision in the Context of Different Drafting Strategies', in G. Rijlaarsdam (series ed.) and L. Allal, L. Chanquoy and P. Largy (vol. eds) *Studies in Writing, Vol. 13. Revision: Cognitive and Instructional Processes* (Dordrecht: Kluwer Academic Publishers), pp. 63–85.

Gall, M. D. (1970) 'The Use of Questions in Teaching', *Review of Educational Research*, 40(5), pp. 707–21.

Gardner, R. C. & Lambert, W.E. (1972) 'Attitudes and motivation in second language learning'. Rowley, MA: Newbury House.

Garrett, N. (2009) 'Computer-assisted Language Learning Trends and Issues Revisited: Integrating Innovation', The Modern Language Journal, 93, pp.719–40.

Gass, S. M., A. Mackey and T. Pica (1998) 'The Role of Input and Interaction in Second Language Acquisition: Introduction to the Special Issue', The Modern Language Journal, 82(3), pp. 299–307.

Gass, S. M. and L. Selinker (2010) Second Language Acquisition: An Introductory Course, 3rd edn (London and New York: Routledge).

Genesee, F., K. Lindholm-Leary, W. Saunders and D. Christian (2005) 'English Language Learners in U.S. Schools: An Overview of Research Findings', Journal of Education for Students Placed at Risk, 10(4), pp. 363–85.

Gilbert, J. B. (2008) Teaching Pronunciation: Using the Prosody Pyramid (Cambridge, UK: Cambridge University Press).

Government of Chile (2014) National English Strategy 2014–2030 (accessed 31 December 2015 from http://www.economia.gob.cl/wp-content/uploads/2014/03/140307-Presentacion-CS-lanzamiento-ENI-v3.pdf).

Grabe, W. (2009) Reading in a Second Language: Moving from Theory to Practice (Cambridge, UK: Cambridge University Press).

Grabe, W. and F. L. Stoller (2002) Teaching and Researching Reading (New York: Pearson Education).

Graddol, D. (2006) English Next, British Council (Plymouth: Latimer Trend & Co.)

Hallman, H. L. (2007) 'Negotiating Teacher Identity: Exploring the Use of Electronic Teaching Portfolios with Preservice English Teachers', Journal of Adolescent and Adult Literacy, 50(6), pp. 474–85.

Hamdan, N., P. McKnight, K. McKnight and K. M. Arfstrom (2013) 'A Review of Flipped Learning', Flipped Learning Network (accessed 15 May 2015 from http://flippedlearning.org/wp-content/uploads/2016/07/LitReview_FlippedLearning.pdf).

Hammersly-Fletcher, L. and P. Orsmond (2005) 'Reflecting on Reflective Practices within Peer Pbservation', Studies in Higher Education, 30(2), pp. 213–24.

Han, Y. J. (2015) 'Successfully Flipping the ESL Classroom for Learner Autonomy', NYS TESOL Journal, 2(1), pp. 98–109.

Harmer, J. (2007) *The Practice of English Language Teaching*, 4th edn (Harlow: Pearson Longman).

Hastings, C. (2012) 'Teacher Motivation: The Next Step in L2 Motivation Research', *TNTESOL Journal*, 5, pp. 61–69.

Hayes, J. R. (2006) Chapter 2: 'New Directions in Writing Research', in C. A. MacAurthur, S. Graham and J. Fitzgerald (eds) *Handbook of Writing Research* (New York: Guilford Press), pp. 28–40.

Healey, D., E. Hanson-Smith, P. Hubbard, S. Ioannou-Georgiou, G. Kessler and P. Ware (2011) *TESOL Technology Standards* (Alexandria, VA: TESOL).

Herreid, C.F. and N. A. Schiller (2013) 'Case Studies and the Flipped Classroom', *Journal of College Science Teaching*, 42(5), pp. 62–66.

Hershatter, A. and M. Epstein (2010) 'Millennials and the World of Work: An Organization and Management Perspective', *Journal of Business and Psychology*, 25(2), pp. 211–23.

Holec, H. (1996) 'Self-Directed Learning: An Alternative Form of Training', *Language Teaching*, 29 (2), pp. 89–93.

Huang, Y. M., T. H. Liang, Y. N. Su, and N. S. Chen (2012) 'Empowering Personalized Learning with an Interactive e-Book Learning System for Elementary School Students', *Educational Technology, Research and Development*, 60(4), pp. 703–22.

Hughes-Hassell and P. Rodge (2007) 'The Leisure Reading Habits of Urban Adolescents', *Journal of Adolescent and Adult Literacy*, 51(1), pp. 22–33.

Ingersoll, R. (2001) 'Teacher Turnover and Teacher Shortages: An Organizational Analysis', *American Educational Research Journal*, 38(3), pp. 499–534.

International Association of Teachers of English as a Foreign Language (IATEFL) (2016) Abstract for Diane Larsen-Freeman's Plenary (accessed 20 April 2016 from https://iatefl.britishcouncil.org/2016/session/plenary-diane-larsen-freeman).

Iverach, L. and R. M. Rapee (2014) 'Social Anxiety Disorder and Stuttering: Current Status and Future Directions', *Journal of Fluency Disorders*, 40, pp. 69–82.

Iwahori, Y. (2008) 'Developing Reading Fluency: A Study of Extensive Reading in EFL. *Reading in a Foreign Language*', 20(1), pp. 70–91.

Jensen, L. (2001) 'Planning Lessons', in M. Celce-Murcia (ed.) *Teaching English as a Second or Foreign Language* (Boston, MA: Heinle & Heinle), pp. 403–13.

Johns, A. M. (2003) 'Genre and ESL/EFL Composition Instruction', in B. Kroll (ed.) *Exploring the Dynamics of Second Language Writing* (Cambridge, UK: Cambridge University Press), pp. 195–217.

K–12 Reader: Reading Instruction Resources (2015) The Relationship between Reading and Writing (accessed 15 December 2015 from http://www.k12reader.com/the-relationship-between-reading-and-writing/).

Karaoglu, S. (2015) 'Motivating Language Learners to Succeed', TESOL International Association (accessed 15 May 2015 from https://www.tesol.org/read-and-publish/journals/other-serial-publications/compleat-links/compleat-links-volume-5-issue-2-(june-2008)/motivating-language-learners-to-succeed).

Kelkar, A. R. (1978) 'Correlative Linguistics', in W. C. McCormack and S. A. Wurm (eds) *Approaches to Language: Anthropological Issues* (Berlin: Mouton), pp. 151–190.

Kellogg, R. T. (2008) 'Training Writing Skills: A Cognitive Developmental Perspective', *Journal of Writing Research*, 1(1), pp. 1–26.

Krashen, S.D (1982) *Principals and Practice in Second Language Acquisition* (New York: Prentice Hall).

Krashen, S. (1996) 'The Case against Bilingual Education', in J. E. Alatis, C. A. Straehle, M. Ronkin and B. Gallenberger, *Georgetown University Round Table on Languages and Linguistics 1996, Linguistics, Language Acquisition, and Language Variation: Current Trends and Future Prospects*, pp. 55–69.

Krashen, S. D. (1998) 'Comprehensible Output', *System*, 26, pp. 175–82.

Krashen, S. D. (2001) *Free Voluntary Reading* (Santa Barbara, CA: Libraries Unlimited).

Krashen, S. D. (2004) *The Power of Reading: Insights from the Research* (Portsmouth, NH: Heinemann).

Kuczynski, B. and S. A. Kolakowsky-Hayner (2011) 'Auditory Discrimination', *Encyclopedia of Clinical Neuropsychology*, pp. 301–302.

Lado, R. (1957). *Linguistics across cultures: Applied linguistics for language teachers*. Ann Arbor, MI: University of Michigan Press.

Langford, C. and J. Albair (2016) 'Teacher-driven Corpus Development: The Online Restaurant Review', presentation, 50th IATEFL Conference, Birmingham, England.

Lantolf, J. P., S. L. Thorne and M. E. Poehner (2014) Chapter 11: 'Sociocultural Theory and Second Language Development', in B. Van Patten and J. Williams (eds) *Theories in Second Language Acquisition: An Introduction* (London and New York: Routledge), pp. 207–26.

Larsen-Freeman, D. (2003) *Teaching Grammar: From Grammar to Grammaring* (Boston, MA: Heinle Cengage Learning).

Larsen-Freeman, D. (2016) Shifting Metaphors from Computer Input to Ecological Affordances,. Plenary at the 50th IATEFL Conference in Birmingham, England.

Latham, N. I., and W. P. Vogt (2007) 'Do Professional Development Schools Reduce Teacher Attrition? Evidence from a Longitudinal Study of 1000 Graduates', *Journal of Teacher Education*, 58(2), pp. 153–67.

Laurillard, D. (2013) Foreword to the first edition, in H. Beetham and R. Sharpe (eds) *Rethinking Pedagogy for a Digital Age* (London and New York: Routledge), pp. xix–xxi.

Lawless, K. A. and J. W. Pellegrino (2007) 'Professional Development in Integrating Technology into Teaching and Learning', *Review of Educational Research*, 77(4), pp. 575–614.

Lehmann, T. and T. Weber (2015) 'English-Teachers' Teaching Perspectives and Their Use of Methods to Foster Students' Communicative Competence: A Comparison between Chile and Germany', *The Journal of Language Teaching and Learning*, 2015-2, pp. 22–36.

Lenhart, A., S. Arafeh, A. Smith and A. R. Macgill (2008) 'Writing, Technology and Teens', Pew Internet and the American Life Project (accessed 15 December 2015 from http://www.pewinternet.org/2008/04/24/writing-technology-and-teens/)

Liu, M., Z. Moore, L. Graham and S. Lee (2002) 'A Look at the Research on Computer-based Technology Use in Second Language Learning: Review of Literature from 1990–2000', *Journal of Research on Technology in Education*, 34(3), 250–73.

Long, M. H. (1996) 'The Role of the Linguistic Environment in Second Language Acquisition', in W. Ritchie and T. Bhatia (eds) *Handbook of Second Language Acquisition* (San Diego, CA: Academic Press), pp. 413–468.

Lumpe, A. T. (2007) 'Research-based Professional Development: Teachers Engaged in Professional Learning Communities', *Journal of Science Teacher Education*, 18(1), pp. 125–128.

Magrath, D. (2016) 'Interference patterns: Applying linguistic theory to lesson production', *TESOL English Language Bulletin*, 12 August 2016. http://exclusive.multibriefs.com/content/interference-patterns-applying-linguistic-theory-to-lesson-production/education.

Magrath, D. (2016) Applying linguistic theory to lesson production. TESOL English Language Bulletin, 12 August 2016 (accessed from http://exclusive.multibriefs.com/content/interference-patterns-applying-linguistic-theory-to-lesson-production/education).

Markus, H. and P. Nurius (1986) 'Possible Selves', *American Psychologist*, 41(9), pp. 954–69.

Mason, B. and S. Krashen (1997) 'Extensive Reading in English as a Foreign Language', *System*, 25(1), pp. 91–102.

McCarthy, M. (2006) *Exploration in Corpus Linguistics* (Cambridge, UK: Cambridge University Press).

McCarthy, M. (2010) 'Spoken Fluency Revisited', *English Profile Journal*, 1(1), pp. 1–15.

Meenakshi (2013) 'Impact of Training through Laboratory on Intonation and Retention of IXth Graders of Kashmir Valley', *International Journal of Linguistics*, 5(2) (accessed 15 May 2015 from Questia research database).

Mercado, L. A. (2012a) *English Language Learning and Technology: Discovering a New Potential* (Boston, MA: Cengage Learning).

Mercado, L. A. (2012b) Chapter 7: 'Guarantor of Quality Building and Assurance', in M. A. Christison and F. Stoller (eds) *A Handbook for Language Program Administrators*, 2nd edn (Miami, FL: ALTA Books).

Mercado, L. A. (2013a) Chapter 3: 'IMMERSE: An Institutional Approach to Pre- and Early-service Teacher Development', in J. Edge and S. Mann (eds) *Innovation in Pre-service Education and Eraining for English Language Teachers* (British Council), pp 47–62.

Mercado, L. A. (2013b) 'Discussant review of K. Beatty, "Beyond the Classroom: Mobile Learning the Wider World"', published online by The International Research Foundation for English Language Education (TIRF) (accessed from http://www.tirfonline.org/english-in-the-workforce/mobile-assisted-language- learning/beyond-the-classroom-mobile-learning-the-wider-world/).

Mercado, L. A. and L. Baecher (2014) 'Video-based Self-observation as a Component of Developmental Teacher Evaluation', *Global Education Review,* 1(3), pp. 63–77.

Mercado, L. A. (2015a) Chapter 10: 'Standards-based Assessment for Young Learners', in C. N. Giannikas, L. McLoughlin and G. Fanning (eds) *Children Learning English: From Research to Practice*, Young Learners and Teenagers Special Interest Group, IATEFL (Reading: Garnett Education), pp. 167–85.

Mercado, L. A. (2015b) Chapter 19: 'Integrating Classroom Learning and Autonomous Learning', in D. Nunan and J. C. Richards (eds) *Language Learning beyond the Classroom* (London: Routledge), pp. 189–200.

Mehisto, P., D. Marsh and M. J. Frigols (2008) *Uncovering CLIL* (New York: Macmillan).

Miller, M. (2014) 'Amazing News: Your Social Media Addiction Might Actually Be Improving Your Writing Skills', *Teen Vogue* (accessed 5 July 2015 from http://www.teenvogue.com/story/texting-social-media-writing-skills).

Mishan, F. (2005) *Designing Authenticity into Language Learning Materials* (Bristol: Intellect Books).

Morgan-Short, K. and H. W. Bowden (2006) 'Processing Instruction and Meaningful Output-based Instruction: Effects on Second Language', *Studies in Second Language Acquisition*, 28, pp. 31–65.

Murphy, J. M. (1991) 'Oral Communication in TESOL: Integrating Speaking, Listening, and Pronunciation', *TESOL Quarterly*, 25(1), pp. 51–76.

Nation, P. (2007) 'The Four Strands', *Innovation in Language Learning and Teaching*, 1(1), pp. 1–11.

Nation, I.S.P. (2008a) *Teaching ESL/EFL Reading and Writing* (London and New York: Routledge).

Nation, I.S.P. (2008b) *Teaching Vocabulary: Strategies and Techniques* (Boston, MA: Heinle Cengage Learning).

Nation, P. and Waring, R. (1997) 'Vocabulary Size, Text Coverage and Word Lists', in N. Schmitt and M. McCarthy (eds) *Vocabulary: Description, Acquisition and Pedagogy* (Cambridge, UK: Cambridge University Press), pp. 6–19.

Navarre Cleary, M. (2014) 'The Wrong Way to Teach Grammar', *The Atlantic*, February (accessed 15 December 2015 from http://www.theatlantic.com/education/archive/2014/02/the-wrong-way-to-teachgrammar/284014/).

Neely, S. (2012) 'Global Business Speaks English', *Harvard Business Review* (accessed 15 May 2015 from: https://hbr.org/2012/05/global-business-speaks-english).

Neves de Jesus, S. and W. Lens (2005) 'An Integrated Model for the Study of Teacher Motivation', *Applied Psychology: An International Review*, 54(1), pp. 119–34.

Niemiec, C. P. and R. M. Ryan (2009) 'Autonomy, Competence, and Relatedness in the Classroom: Applying Self-determination Theory to Educational Practice', *Theory and Research in Education*, 7(2), pp. 133–44.

NCLRC – The Essentials of Language Teaching (2004) Teaching Listening (accessed 15 July 2015 from http://www.nclrc.org/essentials/listening/stratlisten.htm).

Noble, T. (2004) 'Integrating the Revised Bloom's Taxonomy with Multiple Intelligences: A Planning Tool for Curriculum Differentiation', *Teachers College Record*, 106(1), pp. 193–211.

Noels, K. A., L. G. Pelletier and R. J. Vallerand (2000) 'Why Are You Learning a Second Language? Motivational Orientations and Self-Determination Theory', *Language Learning*, 50(1), pp. 57–85.

Nunan, D. (1988) *The Learner-centred Curriculum: A Study in Second Language Teaching* (Cambridge, UK: Cambridge University Press).

Nunan, D. (1999a) *Second Language Teaching & Learning* (Boston, MA: Heinle & Heinle).

Nunan, D. (1999b) Chapter 8: 'Grammar', in D. Nunan (ed.) *Practical English Language Teaching* (New York, NY: McGraw Hill).

Nunan, D. (2003) 'Nine Steps to Learner Autonomy', keynote presentation at the Symposium of the International Association of Teachers of Swedish as a Foreign Language, Stockholm, Sweden.

Nunan, D. (2008) Personal communication in reference to his 2000 study on learner autonomy, made at the 3rd ELT Horizons International Conference in Lima, Peru, June 2008.

Nunan, D. and Richards, J.C. (2015) *Language learning beyond the classroom.* (London and New York: Routledge).

O'Maggio-Hadley, A. (2001) *Teaching Language in Context*, 3rd edn (Boston, MA: Heinle & Heinle).

Oxford Dictionaries Online (OED) (2015) 'Technology' [Defs. 1 & 2] (accessed 27 September 2015 from https://en.oxforddictionaries.com/definition/us/technology).

Packman, A. (2012) 'Theory and Therapy in Stuttering: A Complex Relationship', *Journal of Fluency Disorders*, 37(4), pp. 225–33.

Plester, B., C. Wood and V. Bell (2008) 'Txt Msg n School Literacy: Does Texting and Knowledge of Text Abbreviations Adversely Affect Children's Literacy Attainment?', *Literacy*, 42(3), pp. 137–44.

Popham, W. J. (2001) 'Teaching to the Test', *Educational Leadership*, 58(6), 16–20.

Popham, W. J. (2009) 'Assessment Literacy for Teachers: Faddish or Fundamental?', *Theory Into Practice*, 48, pp. 4–11.

Prensky, M. (2001) 'Digital Natives, Digital Immigrants', *On the Horizon*, 9(5), pp. 1–6.

Prensky, M. (2011) Chapter 2: 'Digital Wisdom and Homo Sapiens Digital', in M. Thomas (ed.) *Deconstructing Digital Natives: Young People, Technology, and the New Literacies* (London and New York: Routledge), pp. 15–29.

Presidency of Uruguay (2015) Programa Ceibal en Inglés por videoconferencia llegó a 600 escuelas urbanas (accessed 15 February 2016 fromhttp://presidencia.gub.uy/comunicacion/comunicacionnoticias/ceibal-ingles-escuelas-ninos-videoconferencia-claudia-brovetto).

Pulgram, E. (ed.). (1954). *Applied linguistics in language teaching.* Washington, DC: Georgetown University Press.

Ray-Subramanian, C. E. (2011) 'Transitional Bilingual Education', in S. Goldstein and J. A. Naglieri (eds) *Encyclopedia of Child Behavior and Development* (Medford, MA: Springer), p. 1501.

Redfield, D. L. and E. Waldman Rousseau (1981) 'A Meta-analysis of Experimental Research on Teacher Questioning Behavior', *Review of Educational Research*, 51(2), pp. 237–45.

Richards, J. C. (2006) *Communicative Language Teaching Today* (Cambridge, UK: Cambridge University Press), pp. 1–46.

Richards, J. C. and C. Lockhart (1997) 'Teacher Development through Peer Observation', *TESOL Journal*, pp. 1–5 (accessed 1 February 2016 from https://www.researchgate.net/profile/Jack_Richards4/publication/234669130_Teacher_Development_through_Peer_Observation/links/5580c02b08ae47061e5f350b.pdf).

Richards, J. C. and T. S. Rodgers (2014) *Approaches and Methods in Language Teaching*, 3rd edn (Cambridge, UK: Cambridge University Press).

Rossell, C. (2005) 'Teaching English through English', *Educational Leadership*, 62(4), pp. 32–36.

Rost, M. (2015) *Teaching and Researching Listening*, 3rd edn (London and New York: Routledge).

Rowlands, I., D. Nicholas, H. R. Jamali and P. Huntington (2007) 'What Do Faculty and Students Really Think about e-Books?', *Aslib Proceedings*, 59(6), pp. 489–511.

Ryan, S. (2006) 'Language Learning Motivation within the Context of Globalisation: An L2 Self within an Imagined Global Community', *Critical Inquiry in Language Studies*, 3(1), pp. 23–45.

Samuels, S. J. (2012) Chapter 1: 'Reading Fluency: Its Past, Present, and Future', in R. Rasinski, C. Blachowicz and K. Lems (eds) *Fluency Instruction: Research-based Best Practices*, 2nd Ed. (New York: The Guildford Press), pp. 7–20.

Schmidt, R. (1993) 'Awareness and Second Language Acquisition', *Annual Review of Applied Linguistics,* 13, pp. 206–26.

Schmitt, N. (2008) 'Instructed Second Language Vocabulary Learning', *Language Teaching Research,* 12(3), pp. 329–63.

Schmitt, N. and M. McCarthy (1997) *Vocabulary: Description, Acquisition and Pedagogy* (Cambridge, UK: Cambridge University Press).

Schön, D. A. (1983) *The Reflective Practitioner: How Professionals Think in Action* (New York: Basic Books).

Schunk, D. H. (1991) 'Self-efficacy and Academic Motivation', *Educational Psychologist,* 26, 207–31.

Schwartz, R. (2001) 'Improving Student-talk-time in the Classroom', presentation, 29 September, ICPNA Binational Center, Lima, Peru.

Scrivener, J. (2005) *Language Teaching: The Essential Guide to English Language Teaching,* 2nd edn (Oxford, UK: Macmillan Education).

Selinker, L. (1972) 'Interlanguage', *International Review of Applied Linguistics in Language Teaching,* 10(1–4), pp. 209–32.

Selivan, L. (2016). *Seventh International ETAI Conference Program Book.* Ashkelon, Israel, July 4–6, 2016.

Sharma, P. and B. Barrett (2007) *Blended Learning* (New York: Macmillan).

Sokolowski, K. and H. Heckhausen (2010) Chapter 7: 'Social Bonding: Affiliation Motivation and Intimacy Motivation', in J. Heckhausen and H. Heckhausen (eds) *Motivation and Action,* 2nd edn (Cambridge, UK: Cambridge University Press), pp. 184–201.

Spada, N. and P. M. Lightbrown (2008) 'Form-focused Instruction: Isolated or Integrated?', *TESOL Quarterly,* 2(2), pp. 181–207.

Spratt, M., G. Humphreys and V. Chan (2002) 'Autonomy and Motivation: Which Comes First?', *Language Teaching Research,* 6(3), pp. 245–66.

Stein, B. and S. Meyer zu Eissen (2006) 'Distinguishing Topic from Genre', in *Proceedings of the I-KNOW '06, Graz,* 6th International Conference on Knowledge Management', *Journal of Universal Computer Science,* pp. 449–56.

Stoller, F. L. (2002) Chapter 10: 'Project Work: A Means to Promote Language and Content', in J. C. Richards and W. A. Renandya (eds) *Methodology in Language Teaching: An Anthology of Current Practice* (Cambridge, UK: Cambridge University Press), pp. 107–23.

Strommen, E. F. and B. Lincoln (1992) 'Constructivism, Technology, and the Future of Classroom Learning', *Education and Urban Society*, 24(4), pp. 466–76.

Swain, M. (1996) 'Discovering Successful Second Language Teaching Strategies and Practices: From Programme Evaluation to Classroom Experimentation', *Journal of Multilingual and Multicultural Development*, 17(2–4), pp. 89–104.

Swain, M. (2000) Chapter 4: 'The Output Hypothesis and Beyond: Mediating Acquisition through Collaborative Dialogue', in J. P. Lantolf (ed.) *Sociocultural Theory and Second Language Learning* (Oxford: Oxford University Press), pp. 97–114.

Taguchi, E., M. Takayasu-Maass and G. J. Gorsuch (2004) 'Developing Reading Fluency in EFL: How Assisted Repeated Reading and Extensive Reading Affect Fluency', *Reading in a Foreign Language*, 16(2), pp. 1–23.

Taguchi, N., N. Naganuma and C. Budding (2015) 'Does Instruction Alter the Naturalistic Pattern of Pragmatic Development? A Case of Request Speech Act', *TESL-EJ*, 19(3), pp. 1–25.

Tan, P.K.W. and R. Rubdy (2008) *Language as Commodity: Global Structures, Local Marketplaces* (London: Continuum International Publishing Group).

Tatsuki, D. (2006) 'What Is Authenticity?', *Authentic Communication: Proceedings of the 5th Annual JALT Pan-SIG Conference*, 13–14 May 2006, Shizuoka, Japan, Tokai University College of Marine Science (accessed 15 May 2015 from https://jalt.org/pansig/2006/HTML/Tatsuki.htm).

Taylor, L. and J. Parsons (2011) 'Improving Student Engagement', *Current Issues in Education*, 14(1) (accessed 15 May 2015 from http://cie.asu.edu/).

TESOL International Association (2016) 'Technology Standards' (accessed 15 January 2016 from https://www.tesol.org/advance-the-field/standards/technology-standards).

Thoonen, E.E.J., P.J.C. Sleegers, F. J. Oort, T.T.D. Peetsma and F. P. Geijsel (2011) 'How to Improve Teaching Practices: The Role of Teacher Motivation, Organizational Factors, and Leadership

Practices', *Educational Administration Quarterly*, 47(3), pp. 496–536.

Thomas, J. W. (2000) *A Review of the Research on Project-Based Learning* (San Rafael, CA: Autodesk Foundation).

Thornbury, S. (n.d.). 'Ed Tech: The Mouse That Roared', *AUS ELT* (accessed 15 May 2015 https://auselt.com/2014/01/15/ed-tech-the-mouse-that-roared-scott-thornbury/

Thornbury, S. (2009) 'Methods, Post-method, and Métodos', Teach English, British Council (accessed 15 May 2015 from https://www.teachingenglish.org.uk/article/methods-post-method-m%C3%A9todos).

United States Department of State (n.d.) *Trace Effects* (accessed 15 April 2016 from http://americanenglish.state.gov/trace-effects).

Ushioda, E. and Z. Dörnyei (2009) Chapter 1: 'Motivation, Language Identities, and the L2 Self: A Theoretical Overview', in Z. Dörnyei and E. Ushioda (eds), *Motivation, Language Identity, and the L2 Self* (Washington, DC: Library of Congress), (pp. 1–8).

Vandergrift, L. (2005) 'Relationships among Motivation Orientations, Metacognitive Awareness and Proficiency in L2 Listening', *Applied Linguistics*, 26(1), pp. 70–89.

Van Patten, B. and T. Cadierno (1993) 'Input Processing and Second Language Acquisition: A Role for Instruction', *The Modern Language Journal*, 77(1), pp. 45–57.

Vernadakis, N., A. Avgerinos, E. Tsitskari and E. Zachopoulou (2005) 'The Use of Computer Assisted Instruction in Preschool Education: Making Teaching Meaningful', *Early Childhood Education Journal*, 33(2), pp. 99–104.

Vescio, V., D. Ross and A. Adams (2008) 'A Review of Research on the Impact of Professional Learning Communities on Teaching Practice and Student Learning', *Teaching and Teacher Education*, 24, pp. 80–91.

Vaughn, R. (December 2015) 'UK among World's Worst for 'Teaching to the Test', Research Finds' (Accessed September 25, 2016 from https://www.tes.com/news/school-news/breaking-news/uk-among-worlds-worst-teaching-test-research-finds).

Villegas, A. M. (2007) 'Dispositions in Teacher Education: A Look at Social Justice', *Journal of Teacher Education*, 58, pp. 370–80.

Volante, L. (2004) 'Teaching to the Test: What Every Educator and Policy-maker Should Know', *Canadian Journal of Educational*

Administration and Policy, 35 (accessed 15 May 2015 from http://files.eric.ed.gov/fulltext/EJ848235.pdf).

Vosloo, S. (2009) 'The Effects of texting on Literacy: Modern Scourge or Opportunity?', *Shuttleworth Foundation*, April, pp. 1–8 (accessed 15 December 2015 from http://citeseerx.ist.psu.edu/viewdoc/download?doi=10.1.1.175.2588&rep=rep1&type=pdf).

Whitehurst, G. J. (2002) 'Scientifically Based Research on Teacher Quality: Research on Teacher Preparation and Professional Development', White House Conference on Preparing Tomorrow's Teachers, 5 March 2002 (accessed 30 January 2016 from http://www.stcloudstate.edu/tpi/initiative/documents/assessment/Scientifically%20Baseds%20Reserach%20on%20Teacher%20Quality.pdf).

Wigfield, A. and J. S. Eccles (2000) 'Expectancy-Value Theory of Achievement Motivation', *Contemporary Educational Psychology*, 25, pp. 68–81.

Wilson, S. M. and J. Berne (1999) 'Teacher Learning and the Acquisition of Professional Knowledge: An Examination of Research on Contemporary Professional Development', *Review of Research in Education*, 24, pp. 173–209.

Wilson, M. and L. E. Gerber (2008) 'How Generational Theory Can Improve Teaching: Strategies for Working with "Millennials"', *Currents in Teaching and Learning*, 1(1), pp. 29–44.

Woody, W. D., D. B. Daniel and C. A. Baker (2010) 'E-books or Textbooks: Students Prefer Textbooks', *Computers & Education*, 55, pp. 945–48.

Yamashita, J. (2013) 'Effects of Extensive Reading on Reading Attitudes in a Foreign Language', *Reading in a Foreign Language*, 25(2), pp. 248–63.

Zohar, A. and Y. J. Dori (2003) 'Higher Order Thinking Skills and Low-Achieving Students: Are They Mutually Exclusive?', *Journal of the Learning Sciences*, 12(2), pp. 145–181.

Index